HOW WE MET

HOW WE MET

STORIES OF LOVE IN THE MODERN AGE

GIANNA PISANO

NEW DEGREE PRESS

HOW WE MET

Stories of Love in the Modern Age

ISBN   978-1-64137-060-8   *Paperback*

ISBN   978-1-64137-061-5   *Ebook*

*To my mom and dad, who taught me to love with
all my heart, and to always give 110%.*

CONTENTS

How unique to this human experience that
we all just wish to be the most important
thing on Earth to someone else.

—TYLER KNOTT GREGSON

INTRODUCTION

———

That old Maryland crab shack really didn't know what was coming.

The year was 1990, and $10 all-you-can-eat crabs was the best deal in Rockville, Maryland... or anywhere in Maryland, for that matter. Old Bay seasoning lingered in the air, and young adults from miles around visited the restaurant on Fridays after work for their fix of the Chesapeake Bay staple.

My dad met my mom while on he was a date with another woman. Okay, that doesn't sound so cute... let me break it down. Basically, my mom and dad both went to the same crab shack one Friday evening, in classic Maryland fashion. My dad saw my mom across the room and instantly knew he would never see another woman so beautiful. But he was with his friends, and she was with hers, so he left without an introduction.

He remembers going home and laying on his bed, thinking of my mom's face, hopelessly staring at the ceiling fan going around and around, and kicking himself for leaving without going up to her. My dad had been in a relationship at the time, and was with her at the crab shack that night. He felt guilty, despite his current unhappy situation, so he never went up to my mom.

That is, of course, until one week later.

By happenstance, they both returned to $10 all-you-can-eat crabs the next Friday. They shared a few side glances across the room, even a flirty wave or two. After making eyes for a while, my dad finally got up and introduced himself, and they pulled their tables together. Their instant connection was apparent to their present company. My mom was with her brother Mike, and her best friend Shelly, who had funnily enough started dating. My dad was with friends from his softball team, probably coming off of a tournament win. Uncle Mike was a contractor and offered to help my dad with his new cable business, and the two exchanged business cards.

"Well, you might as well take our number too, since Mike is always over at our place," my mom daringly chimed in. These were pre-cell phone days, and since Shelly and Uncle Mike had sparked a romance of their own, my mom figured that's where my dad could find him easily. She wrote their phone number down, and my dad gave her his card.

Two more weeks passed. My dad was drowsy on a Friday in his home office. Filing invoices with heavy eyelids, the phone rang. It was my mom, and the rest was history.

A quick engagement, bustling wedding, 25 years of marriage, and four children later, my mom will insist that things haven't changed. My mom still writes "I love you, 110%" on every Anniversary and Valentine's card. My dad is still a softball addict. Nothing can come between the couple, Maryland football, and a crab feast.

They say their only arguments ever revolve around us children. I can't blame them; we're complicated. But as they've grown older and wiser, they've learned to not sweat the small stuff. They've figured out the tough stuff together, like where to live and how to raise their kids.

My dad, when asked about how he met my mom, always smiles: "We've been married for 25 years, and we're still crazy about each other." He insists I get this story perfect; it's *their* story. Whenever he tells it, it's an hour-long ordeal. There will be tears. Every detail will be recounted correctly. He has to get it right.

My parent's love story has made me view love with rose-colored glasses. Having them as role models, and as a guiding example of a healthy relationship, has bred me to be an optimist about love. Relationships can last, if you work at them. Being with one person forever isn't out of the question. Love can last for decades, especially between people like my parents.

Besides, what are the odds of going to the same crab shack two weeks in a row?

110%.

* *

Don't you just love…*love?!*

Whether you met your partner in an organic chemistry lecture during sophomore year of college, or are still searching amidst awkward Tinder and Bumble dates, love and romance strike a chord within many people. We crave the stories of others and are eager to share our own.

With the nationwide divorce rate having dropped to its lowest in 40 years (below 50%), the couples of the world must be doing something right. I fully blame my parents for giving me an optimistic outlook on relationships. When I first heard the story of how my mom and dad met, I cried at the dinner table and vowed to not settle until I found someone who makes me feel the way they feel about each other.

After hearing some particularly sweet love stories, I was incredibly inspired and wanted to hear more. *How We Met* explores serendipitous chance meetings, facts about the love industry, and even some nightmare dates and stories of heartbreak from the boys I swore at the time were *the one.*

How We Met will provide stories of love, lust, and loss surrounding the one thing that brings us all together: human connection.

Whether you're in love or looking for love, most people will admit that at one point or another, they've been inspired by love. I hope that after reading this, you are, too.

So, to the European boy who made me a romantic picnic date in rural Denmark, and then asked me to do his English homework a week later. To my first boyfriend, who taught me so much about what love is (mutual appreciation, dates to Cici's pizza), and what love isn't (jealousy, constant texting, wearing the wrong tie to prom). To every guy I've swiped right to on Tinder, Bumble, or whatever dating app comes next. To the man that I'll someday, eventually end up with:

This one's for you.

SERENDIPITY

MICHELLE AND MARC

Michelle never expected that her love of France and passion for the language would allow her to meet the love of her life.

At the ripe age of 22, Michelle moved to France after college. She studied abroad during her university days, falling in love with the culture, sunny days on the river, and romance filling the Lyon and Paris air. After working for a few years, she stayed in France to get her MBA and worked as an auditor. Her best friend was also living in Paris, and was from Louisiana, just like Michelle. Her best friend was dating a man who happened to be best friends with Marc.

Fast forward, Marc is 29. Michelle—now 28—and him had met a few times, mostly just between mutual friends, but never thought anything of their relationship. After all, Michelle was destined to go back to her home in Louisiana in just three short weeks. Marc was not going to allow it.

At Michelle's going away party, what seemed like a casual encounter soon turned into a romantic getaway. Marc rang the bell to her apartment, grabbed Michelle's suitcase, and swept her off her feet. He simply wouldn't let her go back to the states... not without him, anyways.

"Michelle, you are *it* for me. You always have been," he schmoozed.

Three weeks they spent together, walking the covered bridges, eating pastries, and frolicking along the river Seine—where Marc would ask Michelle to spend the rest of her life with him, at the end of the short 21 days.

Marc officially asked Michelle to marry him on the plane ride back from France to America, so they wouldn't be in either country and could form a union being loyal to both nations.

When Michelle returned home to Louisiana, her father noticed a change... a new spark in his daughter, and certainly a good one. Marc, on the other hand, was nervous. The young couple moved to Kansas, while Marc knew absolutely no English. Their entire relationship thus far had been built in the French language. They even got hitched in a courthouse to make things easier, green card-wise.

Fast forward to today, Marc and Michelle are happily married in Kansas City with three young children. They took the kids to see their favorite spot on a bench along the river Seine a few years ago. Yes, it sounds too good to be true. Sweeter than a macaron, richer than a French wine. But hey, isn't that what love is?

DANNY AND JULIA

Julia was a conservative Jew born in West Orange, New Jersey. Danny was born in Taiwan.

They met in medical school, both studying to be doctors. They sat next to each other at George Washington medical school and got to know each other pretty fast. It was the 80s, a different time period where interracial couples were not as commonplace, and were even frowned upon in some regions of the country. Julia was six years older than Danny. She held a variety of jobs before deciding to be a doctor. They dated for eight years and just decided to get married because they wanted to have kids. Danny's parents disapproved of him dating a white woman, and he was cut off from family. It was a small wedding with a rabbi, and just Julia's parents as two witnesses. After the wedding, they went back to work because they were on call at the hospital. They made x-rays with hearts on it to commemorate their special day in a way only two doctors would.

Fast forward several decades, they have both retired and go on lots of adventures. They have three daughters, and would describe their current state as being "the happiest they've ever been with the best person they could be with." Their sarcasm and shared sense of humor keep their relationship exciting and fun. For example, Danny would say his favorite thing about Julia is her income.

However, their relationship did not come easily. The couple faced backlash from family, friends, and society in general— both because they were an interracial couple and because Julia was six years older. Julia faced judgement from her family about it. And everyone in Danny's family speaks Mandarin, so the language barrier proved to be an instant problem.

One time on one of their first dates, she came down in a casual blue jumper, and he was in a full suit. She had to run up and change. It was a classic, tender, quintessentially *them* moment. They love to tell that story to their children.

It's not often you find two people as truly in love as they are.

"Julia chased me relentlessly until I finally capitulated," Danny jokes.

"I just really love Danny's sense of humor," Julia smiles.

"Yeah? Well I love her hot bod."

KIM AND BILL

Kim and Bill's 31-year marriage is nothing short of #relationshipgoals. I mean, when you meet at a wedding, there are already big shoes (or heels) to fill. As told by Kim:

"The way we met... well, it was funny. I had a roommate, and we were just out of college. My roommate was getting married and I was in the wedding as a bridesmaid. Probably about two months before the wedding, even though they planned it 1.5 years in advance, the groom's sister split up with her husband. Well, she was in the wedding, and he was supposed to be a groomsman. He needed a substitute for the wedding. Fast forward to the wedding day, and my now-husband Bill ends up being the substitute last minute, just a month before the big day. I had never met Bill, but I knew Bill's brother John. We had gone to parties together. John was the best man, and he was good friends with my roommate's fiancé. At the rehearsal dinner was the first time I laid eyes on Bill. We sat next to each other just by chance, despite there being six bridesmaids and six groomsmen. We went and had dinner and sat next to each other. We started talking. There was definitely a physical attraction, but we also really liked each other and he was really funny and I liked that about him right away.

The wedding was the next day. Afterwards, we started dancing at the reception and he asked me to dance. He was funny and fun. He seemed to have his act together. At the end of the reception he asked me to go to a party, but I had already been asked to go somewhere else with another gentleman, so I couldn't go with Bill. A really good quality of his was that he was really confident. He kept saying things like 'You will have a MUCH better time with my friends and I, so come with me.' He was persistent in a nice way, and I liked it. I canceled with the other guy and went with Bill. We went on two dates. He called me, and didn't even wait until Saturday night; he called me the next day. 'I want to see you again. Let's get drinks on Tuesday,' he said. I liked that he didn't have a game or agenda. He wasn't thinking, 'Oh, I can't see her until a few days.' So we went out two or three times, still while the bride was on the honeymoon in Bermuda. When she came back, I told her that she would never guess who I'm dating…the groomsman, Bill! She was shocked, and this is the best part: said she never would have thought to fix us up. They only stayed married a year and a half, and Bill and I continued to date for about another year and a half. He proposed another year and a half after that.

I love how even as we get older, and we have two grown children now, we still have fun and are attracted to each other. Things aren't always easy, though. You know people get sick, and both Bill's parents passed away last year. We've been married 31 years and he is still my best friend. We complement each other as we've gotten older. There's a big respect factor. When he's at a low point, I'm there to bring to him up. He didn't get a college degree, because he had to come home from school for personal reasons and had to take care of his mom, so he went back to school when I was pregnant with our first daughter, Lindsay. You have to be selfless. There are times he gets on my nerves, but you just kind of have to realize that nobody's perfect. But I feel pretty lucky and blessed that I have someone who lets me be *me*. We have an incredible trust. He makes me the best person I can be."

Kim is just about finished describing her and Bill's romance, when she realizes there's one very special detail she left out.

"I almost forgot the corniest part of the whole story! At the reception, and I'm not lying, I caught the one and only bouquet I've ever caught in my life. Even after being a bridesmaid at six weddings. And Bill? He caught the garter."

ILY AND JAIME

"I'm 51, Jaime is 53. We've been together for 34 years," Ileana says. Their love story, ridden with ups and downs, complicated love across country borders, and a fair share of dramatic events, has stood the test of time. Now, it's the real deal.

"We met at a supermarket when I was 17, and he was 19. It was the day I arrived in the United States for my study abroad program in August, in Los Angeles. I was an exchange student from Mexico for the year. Jaime worked at the supermarket, usually in the milk and dairy section. I remember seeing him that day, paying at the register, and him going to cash and pick up his check," she recalls.

After that, it just so happened that he was a close friend of her host family. She was expected to go to Hawaii after her sister went to Hawaii for an exchange program, and loved her host family. But Ileana picked LA because she didn't want to be on an island, but rather on the mainland United States. She was there for a year. Jaime was friends with her host family, and really good friends with her host sister.

"Basically after the day that I first met him, I would go back to the supermarket every time we needed milk. I would always offer to go to the market for my family, and he was always working in the dairy section. It as a routine. The funniest part is, I don't even like milk," she laughs.

"About 10 days later, I got invited to what happened to be his best friend's birthday party, and that's where we were officially introduced. It was August. We started talking, and we started dating in December. By the end of April, my study abroad was over and I went back to Mexico to go to college. That was 1984. We saw each other in 1984, 85, 86... but there was another guy trying to date me back in Mexico. I started dating this other guy, but I was still in close contact with Jaime in LA. At one point, I even visited him, but he was applying to graduate school so he was stressed and didn't want to get too serious. We kept in touch and talked all the time. We constantly wrote letters to each other, even though I was still dating the guy from Mexico," Ileana continues.

Then, it was Jaime's turn to visit Ileana, but he bailed last minute and ended up not coming. They got in a big argument. Next thing you know, things got more serious with Ileana's boyfriend in Mexico. She got engaged to another guy. Jaime then disappeared for about a year, and he didn't even know about the engagement.

One day, Jaime called Ileana and said told her that he was ready to finally be together. This is when she broke the news that she was engaged. The year was 1990. Jaime insisted on seeing her, and she agreed, but her small town in Mexico was hard to access. Plus, everyone would see her in public with another man who wasn't her fiancé. As a solution, they packed their bags for a weekend away in another town. Even though Ileana wore the engagement ring from her fiancé, she knew that marriage was not going to happen. At the end of their weekend getaway, Jaime gave her an ultimatum: choose someone.

Ileana found this simple. "When Jaime asked me this, he definitely didn't know that I had made up my mind to not marry the other guy. It was always him. It was always Jaime."

Back in her Mexico hometown, Ileana realized things were not as simple. Besides, she had a fiancé that she somehow needed to break up with.

She continues with their story: "Jaime dropped me off at the airport and I told him I needed time to sort things out back at home. My fiancé and I had already had opened an account to buy the furniture for our new house. At the time, I owned decoration store, so I had to use some funds from that account to put a down payment on the furniture. My fiancé got mad and started yelling and screaming because I took the money from the account. Luckily for me, though, he gave me the scapegoat, and called the engagement off. It wasn't over yet, though, because Jaime didn't know I broke up with him. Jaime then broke up with ME... so I went back to my hometown with no boyfriend or wedding or anything. It was heartbreaking.

That May, I was talking to my dad and he was saying that he could tell I was so sad and depressed from breaking up with my fiancé, but in reality I was sad from Jaime. My dad knew about Jaime; he basically knew there was a guy in the United States. I called Jaime and I asked him if he had one wish in the world in the world, what would it be? I of course was hoping he would say he wish was to see me. And sure enough, he said it.

I hopped on a plane to LA, and he hits me with the kicker: he had a girlfriend! I was shocked, but could see his smug smile. He was just kidding and wanted to give me a taste of my own medicine! From then, it all happened quickly. We got engaged 3 months later. We went back to Mexico and got married in September."

Ileana says the best thing about their relationship is that it hasn't changed. "I mean, we had three children, we had to grow up, he had work, and I was taking care of the kids. But we always try to at least have a date night. As crazy as it sounds to both of us, every time we want to kill each other, we go back to our story."

After going through so much to be together, the couple likes to put things into perspective and look at the love that they fought so long and hard for.

JACKIE AND JD

Over 25 years later, not much has changed for Jackie and JD (also known as John Dillon, but if you meet him, you'll agree: he's *totally* a JD). They have an amazing group of friends who love bowling and meeting up at the neighborhood steakhouse, two children—who are grown themselves, at 24 and 21—and a love that everyone should strive for.

"We met through our friends, Tony and Cathy. Cathy introduced me to him. When Tony opened his pizza parlor, a pizza delivery place off Snouffer School Road in Maryland, I was working with Tony and Cathy in the mortgage business. At his shop's grand opening, JD was there. We met briefly, just for a few seconds, and I wasn't even there that long because I had a date that night. We didn't really exchange numbers…but we saw each other again at a bar called Chasers a few weeks later. I knew he was going to be there. We've been together ever since. He proposed at Ben and Jerrys, on my birthday in 1991."

It was the 90s, after all. No Facebook, Instagram, or even email. Now, it's so easy to find someone's online persona and shoot them a message. It was more common back then to meet through friends, or have a serendipitous exchange, like seeing each other at the same bar a few weeks after meeting. It's those little winks from the Universe that make crazy ideas like *fate* seem a bit more possible.

Even now, a quarter of a decade later, things still feel as electric as the very first day.

Jackie agrees that things have stayed the same: "Our relationship hasn't really changed. We certainly grow together as one person, and make our decisions together. We are pretty much on the same page on a lot of things: raising the kids, our goals in life, what our interests are. Luckily we've never really disagreed on much, that's for sure. We've had a pretty easy time, except for life's tougher moments. JD's parents passed on, as did my mother. Our son Nick was diagnosed with diabetes, which was rough for a little while."

On an average weekend, you could find Jackie and JD tailgating for a football game with their closest friends, many of whom have been close to the couple since they first met (Tony and Cathy included). They might be walking their two adorable dogs, or driving to their beach condo in Ocean City, Maryland. Their shared interests make every day a new adventure, even though they're both just as happy cozying up on the couch. An innate romantic, JD might surprise Jackie with a bouquet of flowers, or a meal at her favorite restaurant. And of course, no day is complete for the couple without a few rounds of side-splitting laughter.

Jackie even giggles as she says this. "My favorite thing about JD is that he makes me laugh. We laugh a lot, and we can be together all the time. I never feel like I can't be with him, like I need to get away from him. We can talk about anything."

DON AND NADINE

"How we met... well, we've been married 28 years and I don't even know how to sum it up," Nadine smiles. She's been with her husband Don for almost three decades, but is still trying to find the right words to say to describe their love. She does call it "the best story ever," though.

Don and Nadine worked in the same office, both as retail buyers. At the office there were a lot of young people, and they would all go out to happy hour after work. They shared a group of "work friends" and spent a lot of time together with them. This is when their connection sparked.

"We started dating, but we actually kept it a secret because our office only had about 50 people. We worked in the same department, but we didn't know if there were any policies about dating so we kept it secret, and it was not easy to keep it secret. We lived in NYC and, believe it or not, as big as

NYC is, you become very to localized where you live and the restaurants you frequent. We knew where everyone lived, so we had to avoid certain places because we didn't want people to find us out," Nadine describes.

It really is a small world after all. Nadine knew that people always caught trains at Penn Station on Fridays, so the pair would avoid that area to not run into their coworkers. They describe it as "extremely calculated."

Nadine continues: "There were a lot of instances where if I was staying at his apartment, we wouldn't walk into the office together. One of us would go get a coffee beforehand. We were so secretive that nobody ever found us out! But one day we decided to let the cat out of the bag. We came in and talked to our boss and told him that we were engaged. It was quite the uproar in the whole office, and people couldn't even work because they were so shocked and excited for us. It was really fun. They threw us a great shower, and we invited friends from our office down to Maryland for our wedding."

Switching from a city life in New York City to a suburban style in Maryland was no simple transition. Things got even more hectic with the arrival of their two children, Ryan and Emily. The couple, accustomed to doing fun things together with their plethora of shared interests, now had to divide time and attention with their kids.

While their love remained strong and intact, a new normal was developed. "We were married for six years before we had any kids. We loved that time and traveled a lot, tried a lot of new restaurants, and hung out with our friends in NYC and New Jersey. Then we moved to Maryland, which is where we still live. We went to a lot of events and concerts, visited the theater, and did so many fun things together. We thought that was a great time to enjoy ourselves as a couple. Then we had our children, and I stayed home from work. Moves can be hard to go through. Don took a new job in Maryland and I was still in NYC working there, and we would commute on weekends back and forth, up and down the East coast. We knew that was temporary and wouldn't work for long, because long distance was not our thing. I finally got a job in DC, so we lived under the same roof. When we moved to Maryland, the kids came shortly thereafter. That was an interesting transition of roles. We were always together so much, living in New York, commuting together, going out to dinner together…and then I took the traditional housewife mom role, cooking dinner for the very first time. Don was always the cook," Nadine says, laughing.

Becoming a mom was a big transition for Nadine, because it was a new role for her, but one that she always wanted. She states that it wasn't easy being a stay-at-home mom, and immersed herself in activities to combat the challenge. While Don was at work, Nadine took the kids to the library for story time, and visited every single park in a 10-mile radius. She took on a very active mom role, scheduling a lot of playdates for Ryan and Emily.

Switching gears from working full-time to being the ultimate mom, time really flew by right in front of Nadine's eyes, she says. "I think there was a chunk of time that passed by, that the kids were young and then all of a sudden they're in high school. It felt like a blur, even though at the time it didn't feel like that. As parents we were supporting their events and sports and music. We did everything as a family. For 18 years, Don and I supported everything our kids did. I joined the PTA. We did fundraising for their sports teams. We became stronger as a couple by dedicating our life to Ryan and Emily."

Nadine says that's why it feels like a blur: their kids' agendas became their agendas. Their friends became the parents of their kids' friends. And now, as empty-nesters with a 22-year-old and a 20-year-old, Don and Nadine finally remember what it's like to be a couple again. They travel on weekends, go out to dinner on a random Wednesday night if they feel like it, and have started cooking meals together. No more "divide and conquer" mindset. Now, they're in it together.

But despite any challenges or changes that crossed their path, Don and Nadine remained a happy couple. Both have laundry lists of what they love most about the other. Nadine starts:

"my favorite thing about Don…well, he is a gourmet cook. That is the biggest bonus to me. He is very easy to live with and be with. I've never lived with other men, but I hear horror stories. He is very easy tempered. We like the same activities, so that's awesome because we are very compatible. I like that he's a great father and a good head of the household. He takes care of all of us. I like that he has a responsible job. He is no slacker. I like that we share our faith together."

Don chimes in now, agreeing: "The compatibility is my favorite thing about Nadine, because we do well together. I cook, she cleans. That we do really well," he laughs. He loves how she is always excited about stuff, whether it be their kids, or a meeting at school, or a new hobby. "She's very high energy, which is a positive trait. She's really smart, so we can compete in minds. We share a common faith, which is important to us. I like that she's independent. She's not afraid to go do what she wants to do. I guess there's a lot of trust there…if she wants to hang out with her friends, or take a vacation, she goes for it."

Trust and positivity is their formula for keeping relationships long-term. The couple's shared interests allow every day to bring something new. Don even admits that he doesn't have Nadine completely figured out, but it keeps him on his toes.

As for their humble beginnings, neither Don nor Nadine could imagine their relationship without being friends first.

"We were friends for a long time before we started dating, which is where our longevity comes from," Don states. "We started as friends, and that's how it's stayed for 30 years."

PAOLO AND VANESSA

Some say that print journalism is dead. But for others, it made their love come to life.

Vanessa and Paolo have been dating for a year and a half, but more than half that time has been apart. They met while working for their university's school newspaper, and Paolo was the editor for Vanessa's work. But just when their love began to spark, Vanessa was set to study abroad in Europe. Timing's a bitch, as they say.

Vanessa recalled the story with a sweet smile, "We were both in same section on the school newspaper, and it was the summer before junior year. I was going abroad, about to spend the whole year abroad in Scotland. Before the end of sophomore year, he reached out to me as the incoming sports section editor to see how involved I wanted to be at the newspaper while going abroad. I had never interacted with Paolo before, and I actually thought he was Italian based on his name. He's actually Filipino," she laughed. "I went into the newspaper's office on campus, and he was there, and right away I thought, 'wow, this is not what I expected at all.' He was really cool, really nice, and REALLY cute. I had a feeling, I remember, that 'Oh, this guy's important.' In the summer he reached out to me around May after sophomore year. I don't know why he reached out. It might have been about a summer column. He asked me if I wanted to write a sports column during the summer. I kept the conversation going by talking about sports. We like different hockey teams, which caused a bit of conflict," she smiled. "We started talking a lot. I liked Paolo, but there was actually another girl in the picture at the time. I was totally in the friend-zone. I didn't realize that Paolo was into me…that part took a while."

Paolo's point of view is just as love-ridden and just as seren-dipitous. He never communicated with Vanessa that after sophomore year was over, the other girl was out of the picture. It had never been anything serious, anyways, just a few casual dates. He was a single man, but Vanessa thought it was more serious than that. Not to mention that Paolo hadn't updated his relationship status on Facebook or anything, so the general public was not in the know. When Vanessa came into the newspaper office at the end of their sophomore year, it was the last night of production for that current staff. Paolo was getting ready to take over the position of sports editor, and it was causing him a great deal of stress.

"The second she walked in, she was such a breath of fresh air. For starters, she was adorable," Paolo blushed.

"Vanessa was just so cute, so bubbly and smiley. An instant mood boost. My friends were saying how cute she was, and kept saying she was so nice and that they were all so glad that she was in the sports section as a writer this semester. I agreed with them. We started officially 'talking' over the summer, but we mostly had casual conversations. I noticed that I was being very flirty with her, but not even intentionally, just subconsciously. We talked for a little bit, about a month, and I realized that I actively liked her. We would talk on the phone casually, and one day I decided to pick up the flirting a little bit more and see if she was interested."

This is when the "friend-zone" really kicks in. Paolo asked her to get dinner and to watch sports together, and Vanessa thought, "Wow, this guy is such a good friend." He really liked her, and one day told her straight away. He told her, "I really like you, and I like talking to you, and I don't know how you really feel about this, but here you go."

It's at this moment that we all realize how truly romantic Paolo is. He sent her a list of eight things he liked about her.

> 1) you're adorable
> 2) you convinced me to watch GoT (big plus)
> 3) you are so sweet and so kind
> 4) you said you'd go to an nba game with me
> 5) you convinced me that getting butterflies is still a thing
> 6) you make me happier than should be humanly allowed from like two thousand miles away
> 7) you have made me legitimately believe that the worst darkness is bearable because of the amazing light you find at the end of it
> 8) you laugh at my dumb jokes and say all the weird stuff i do too

Paolo cringed while retelling this. "Vanessa is usually a really good texter, and will always respond within a few minutes. But this time she didn't respond for around 25 minutes. I thought it was all over, that I totally blew it. Then she sends the sweetest text ever with 9 things she liked about me. She one-upped my meager list of 8. It was then very clear that we liked each other, but she was leaving the country to go abroad, so we had to get serious. She understood if I wanted to see other people, but I know she was secretly hoping I wouldn't say that. It was killing her that she wouldn't be on campus with me, since I wanted to go on dates and really fall for each other in the Fall! We felt something and wanted to give it a shot. I knew the year would be crazy because of my editor position at the newspaper, and I had a good feeling about this girl. I remember thinking, 'If this girl is as good as I think she is, we can make it long distance. We would do it the right way, be healthy about it, have good times in our respective locations, but still keep in touch. It was a very 2017 relationship: super digital. Our only interactions before that were as friends through the newspaper. We really wanted to take it to another level."

Because they started as friends through a shared interest, it took some time for Vanessa to get beneath the surface and realize that Paolo really liked her. She thought she was in the friend-zone and didn't know if he was still with anyone, but when she found out he was single, a switch inside of her flipped. They started dating that summer, and while she was studying abroad and decided to come to campus after months of long distance.

"We were both sad, and I was 5 hours ahead of him because of the time difference," Vanessa explains. "He was always busy in a typical junior year fashion, so I looked into plane tickets for October because I was going to come for spring break. I found a really good ticket and asked him what he thought about me flying to the States for a visit. He told me it had to be a joke, telling me there was no way I'd buy the ticket. But I did," she said.

"Yep, it was October 14-23, 2016. Best week ever," Paolo smiled.

"You remember the dates?!" Vanessa laughed.

"I mean, we spent every second together and just talked for a week straight. She finally met my friends, and our first official date was at Carmine's in Chinatown. It's a really good Italian-style family restaurant. I still remember what we ate, too. We had pesto pasta, and then cupcakes and coffee for dessert because we both really love coffee," Paolo recalled.

After a tumultuous time apart, and then an equally emotional semester together, the couple has begun to navigate life in the same space. Life's little crossovers begin to happen, and a comfort level with one another becomes the norm.

"Now we have the physical component to our relationship, since we were apart for a year. We still Skyped everyday, but it was hard because he was always so tired from working at the newspaper, and my time difference would add confusion, too," Vanessa added.

"We Skyped pretty much everyday. I think we missed 4 days during the school year while Vanessa was gone," Paolo noted. They smiled, proud of their accomplishment. Despite final exams and an ocean dividing them, they beat one of the greatest challenge that couples face: being in a relationship with your computer screen.

As far as favorite things about one another, Paolo and Vanessa had no shortage of things to say. A long list of loves, a confession of compliments: "I'll start," Paolo said proudly. "So college can often have an infamous busy culture where people are always busy and no one has any time to go do anything. But I love how Vanessa is up for whatever. She will be willing to go on an adventure, to do anything. Some days we will have an hour before class and we will go to a coffee shop. We try to make weekday date nights a thing. We tried to do a weekly burger outing but we ended up ditching the schedule and just going all the time. We built a rhythm, but she will always surprise me."

And of course, their love story would not be complete without some sports talk. "Vanessa loves sports, which is a big thing for me. It's a big deal in my life, and people from home say they can't believe I found a girlfriend who's so into sports! She's always there for me, even in the littlest ways. We love surprises, and just the other day Vanessa surprise me with a new pair of Bose wireless headphones that I had been wanting. And she goes beyond just the surprises and big moments, but the smaller moments, too. Just her being there, asking how I am, making time to give me a hug, asking me if I have anything going on...even when she's busy, too! She is an economics major, and she is always working, but she still always goes out of her way to make sure I have someone to talk to if I need anything."

"Yeah, we really love surprises," Vanessa added. "My favorite thing about Paolo is how genuine he is. I feel like people often pretend to be someone they're not, but he is always himself. He is so nice. I see it all the time, and I joke that we can't go anywhere nearby without Paolo running into 3 people he knows. You can tell he genuinely cares about them, too. He asks more than the classic, 'Hey how are you?' I also love his bromance with his best friend Evan. He is such a loyal friend to everyone. He came and visited me this summer and made a point to really get to know my family and my little sister. Paolo and my dad are really bros. They got margaritas together, they bro hug when they see each other, and I'm grateful for their relationship. Paolo is always truly himself, and I really like that about him."

"When Vanessa met my parents, that was a big moment for me. They get along great, and my puppy *loves* Vanessa. I hadn't met any of her family, and her mom was in DC for a conference one time, so I asked to meet up with her during that. I got dinner with just her mom, having never met her before. It went great. It was awesome. I was so nervous, but it went well, and her mom is super genuine just like her. The first thing she said was that it was clear I loved her very much. I was so happy when she said that," Paolo said. Vanessa smiles, noting how happy that made her. The fact that he went out of his way to meet her mom showed how much he cared.

Where are they now? Well, it's safe to say things are smooth sailing. Dating is easy when you live a 10-minute walk apart.

"Here we are now, in senior year of college. In the past, we had a tried and true routine to Skype and catch up on the day and share fun moments, and then one of us would have to go, and we'd text until someone fell asleep. This year, she gets home from her schedule around 6pm, and we make dinner together, usually eating leftovers the next day," Paolo added.

Vanessa giggled, "He doesn't even like leftovers!"

BY THE NUMBERS

THE L WORD

He told me he loved me after three months.

I was taken aback by his abrupt confession, half-hoping to pause time to think of a coherent answer, and half-hoping I suddenly had to pee, or take an urgent phone call. Anything to get me out of there. I even considered bolting and trying to get stuck in the elevator of my dingy freshman dorm, a daunting idea to someone as claustrophobic as myself. But still, nothing was as daunting as being told 'I love you' for only the *third* time in your life (besides family, of course) in the *second* semester of your *first* year of college. A modern-day nightmare of a countdown.

It takes a year to fully know someone enough to tell them you love them, according to psychobiological couples expert Stan Tatkin. "Very soon, people begin to automate each other just like riding a bicycle, and you stop thinking about them so intensely. It's normal so your brain can free up resources for new novelty," he says.

Biology has it all planned out, you see. Nature's plan is for us to partner up and procreate. In fact, nature wants us to shack up together so badly that chemicals in our brain will completely disregard the things that are "wrong" with people. Testosterone tells us to disregard asymmetries in the face, which detracts us from one another. Then serotonin brings the daydreams, that "can't stop thinking about you" type of feeling.

"The general plan that nature has is about four years, which is believed to be long enough to have and raise a child before both parties part ways and find another partner. That's what nature wants—the constant mixing of genes," Tatkin notes.

Our brains are always on the hunt for something new and fresh, and apparently, so are our hearts. I had just gotten out of a long-term relationship. I was just starting college, and my love for the constant changes occurring in my life was as unrequited as my love for him.

Some of life's craziest decisions take guts. I mean, this guy told me he loved me after three months, after all. But it sure took guts for me to not say it back.

LET'S TALK ABOUT SEX

SEX. Now that I have your attention...

It's no secret that sex is a vital aspect of a healthy relationship. In fact, humankind has evolved such that for the first time in history, humans are experiencing sexuality not just to reproduce and have a bunch of children. Rather, "this is the first time in the history of humankind that we want sex simply for the pleasure and connection that is rooted in desire," teaches Esther Perel at her TED Talk about how sex is the secret to desire in a long-term relationship. It's the squeaky wheel, the one thing that might need fixing.

"So we come to one person, and we basically are asking them to give us what once an entire village used to provide. Give me belonging, give me identity, give me continuity, but give me transcendence and mystery and awe all in one. Give me comfort, give me edge. Give me novelty, give me familiarity. Give me predictability, give me surprise," Perel says. We beg for it from our significant others. We need it all from one person. And if we can't have it, we keep looking, onto the next one. Sex is what maintains the intimacy; it's only between you two. Sex separates your best friends from your boyfriends or girlfriends, or husbands or wives. You can have an incredibly intimate emotional connection with someone, but if they aren't a sexual partner, it's one step down the ladder from this idea of a "perfect love."

"Because in some way one could say sex isn't something you do. Sex is a place you go. It's a space you enter inside yourself and with another, or others," Perel states. But where you go, and the parts you connect, is entirely up to you. Everyone has unique expression of themselves, and a different sexual partnership with another person.

"Sex isn't just a behavior. It's a language."

How straight couples met their partners

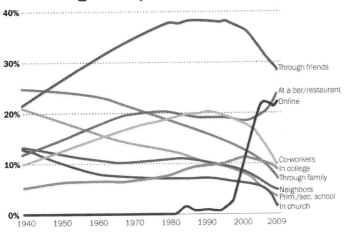

WAPO.ST/**WONKBLOG**
Source: Searching for a Mate: The Rise of the Internet as a Social Intermediary

Washington Post reporter Roberto Ferdman warns us that there are only three people to meet someone anymore. He gives us a few key points about love that are well-known in today's changing society.

First, people are getting married older. Second, you probably live in close proximity to the person you are going to end up with. This is usually attributed to densely populated urban areas.

Third, and most striking, is the way that modern couples meet. Most popular over the years, although declining in the past decade, is meeting through friends. The classic mutual friend situation encompasses many sweet love stories. Around 30% of couples meet this way. Coming in second, and on the rise, is at a bar or restaurant. A contrived social environment is a breeding ground for new couples, or at least a one-night stand or two. And third, the kicker: online. The percentage of couples who met online is growing exponentially, even more pronounced in same-sex couples. Nearly one in three relationships begin online.

"This data reflects the urbanization of society, which has inflated the role of bars and restaurants in courtship. In 1940, only about 57% of the population lived in cities. Over time, however, that number has only shot up, reaching 81% of people living in cities in 2010," Ferdman states.

The role of family and co-workers is rapidly declining, too. Church is hardly even on the chart because so few people are meeting there. These smaller circles we run in are no longer the means to finding an end. And it's mostly thanks to the World Wide Web.

"Now that our lives are no longer sparse, we don't lean quite so heavily on the mini communities we have historically looked to for companionship. The drop in primary and secondary school matchmaking is indicative of the rising age of marriage. And there's the Internet—most of the above trends can be attributed, at least partly, to its rise."

So if you're looking for love, try to find it through friends, at a bar, or online. Besides, that's what everyone else is doing.

LOVE IS CHEMICAL

Maybe Rihanna wasn't too far off with her song "Love on the Brain." It's all chemical, after all. It starts and end in our brain. Love is hearts and Valentine's Day and first dates, but love is also neurons; constant communication and sending messages between cells that we can't begin to control. These messages tell our body how to react when Jake from math class walks in, or Stacy finally texts back with two heart-eye emojis. These messages are nonstop, sometimes conflicting, and always emotion-inducing. Love is physical and emotional, but most importantly, it's chemical.

Helen Fisher tells us in her TED Talk "Why we love, why we cheat" that there are two main characteristics of romantic love. The first is craving. We crave people sexually (ex: I want your body, and I want it now), but also emotionally (ex: I want you to invite me to dinner and ask me about my childhood). These unique combinations of cravings that someone has for another can comprise their unique love.

The second characteristic is motivation: "The motor in the brain begins to crank, and you want this person." It becomes an obsession, that all-day-and-night-thinking-about-some-one-else type of feeling. You're motivated by the possibility of John asking you out to the Cheesecake Factory next Friday. Maybe you're motivated by the red heart next to his name on Snapchat, or the 56-day streak of sending meaningless photos back and forth. It could be a totally contrived scenario in your head of you and *insert name of the apple of your eye* retiring to your California King bed at the end of a long day. You don't know if it will ever occur, but there's a small, improbable possibility that it will.

And that's enough to keep you on your toes.

THE PUBLIC EYE

When your relationship is in the public eye, many people will have their own opinions on it. When rapper Offset proposed to rapper Cardi B onstage at a concert in Philadelphia in October 2017, fans sounded off almost instantly. Cardi B has made headlines in 2017 for her hit song *Bodak Yellow*, so when rapper Offset presented to her a huge teardrop diamond ring, audiences everywhere (especially Twitter) fired up their typing fingers. People felt the proposal was too public, imper-sonal, and even a bit staged. Some people thought the entire romance was motivated by their financial situations, while some fans were thrilled for the happy couple. Speculation ensued that the entire marriage was a sham. Who are we to criticize the relationships of celebrities? There are countless case studies of successful Hollywood relationships, as well as marriages falling apart.

Shows like The Bachelor and Bachelorette are clearly manufactured, but wonderfully entertaining at the same time. Viewers know the love is fake, but glorify it anyways. Fan bases grow, couple obsession becomes real, and the public eye's vision becomes a sharp 20-20. When it comes to having opinions on the love between two people, suddenly everyone is tuned in. Viewers can even nominate their own friends to be the next contestant, and I'd be lying if I said I never tried to get my best friend on the air. A girl can dream!

Other celebrities are no exceptions, either. Who remembers Kim Kardashian's infamous 72-day marriage to Kris Humphries? While their relationship could have been contrived from the beginning, it didn't stop media outlets from sprouting up rumors of cheating, talks of business deals, and accusations of getting married just to boost show ratings. All of which may very well be true, and a horrible standard of celebrity marriages was set during this 2012 summer, but the truth might never be spilled.

We idolize 90s iconic couples like Winona Ryder and Johnny Depp. Their chic style and blasé "we don't really care about the paparazzi" attitude won them fame, which may have been what they were after all along. Justin Timberlake and Britney Spears, denim-clad and back in action, won over the hearts of fans but couldn't keep their love going for as long as the media was after them. And of course, there was the earth-shattering divorce of Brad Pitt and Angelina Jolie, whose ten-year relationship filled with fame, movies, and six children blew up seemingly overnight under the media's fine-tuned microscope.

Any love that's in the spotlight is sure to undergo criticism. Celebrities, individuals holding a position in office, or even individuals who receive media attention all get their limelight, whether they want it or not.

Whether or not pop culture is indicative of what love is really like, we will still be tuned into TV sets every Monday night, just hoping to get that Bachelor's Final Rose.

A FRESH START

"My mom divorced my dad who constantly cheated on her and now she out here living her best life in Cabo with a new boo who takes her places."

When in doubt, find a significant other who appreciates you.

Never have I believed this more than when I saw this Tweet, where a complete stranger recounts her mother's bravery for divorcing her deadbeat, cheating husband and finding a new man who wines and dines her. It's never too late to start over. First marriages aren't always the charm, and sometimes all it takes is a small reminder in 140 characters or less. It went viral, attracted over 240,000 retweets and likes from fans of the happy couple, pictured on a boat off the coast of an island. Their new adventure seemed to be just beginning.

Why is it that the smallest of love stories can contain the most hope? It could be all of the unknowns, or the simple silhouette into the life of a happy new couple. It's truly never too early to start over and find someone new. Go for the person that will make you feel things you've never felt, see thing you've never seen, and do things you've never done. Love is an adventure, and it helps to find someone who's along for the ride.

I recently ran into my favorite high school teacher at the mall. Amidst eye-rolls from customers as a result of our incredibly loud reunion inside Madewell, she told me she was getting married in a few weeks...for the *third* time. She seemed ecstatic, buzzing, and not at all worried about what anyone thought of her.

"I mean, when your first husband refuses to dance with you at your wedding, you need to take that as a red flag," she explained, laughing under her breath. "And then when your second husband makes you so mad that you kick a door and go into your high school classes that week limping, that's also a bad sign." Her candor and openness emphasized just how happy she clearly was now, nearing 50 with two grown children. She was marrying an Italian man in a winter wedding, just days after Christmas. It was a small and intimate ceremony, with elegant details hand-selected by the couple. Pulling up her Pinterest page in the middle of the store, she made sure to assure me that they had the exact same taste. She was positive that third time was the charm; he was "the one." I haven't seen or spoken to her since, but I'd like to believe she's happy. If anyone deserves it, she does.

After being cheated on, lied to, or disrespected by an ex, what do you *possibly* have to lose from a fresh start?

Spoiler alert: nothing. You've got nothing to lose.

YOUR COMBINATION OF ORDINARY

"What people care deeply about and cherish and talk to their therapists most about and fall madly in love with you over is actually your particular combination of ordinary," therapist Katherine Schafler states.

Think about the last person you loved. It could be a romantic love, strictly platonic, or somewhere in between. What do you love most about that person?

Chances are, it's actually quite boring. Some examples from Schafler, who was formerly Google's in-house therapist:

"My son's laugh. How he rests the TV remote on his belly. The way she knows exactly what she wants to order at The Cheesecake Factory, but ends up eating off my plate. When she walks right into my house and raids the pantry without warning, no formal ask required."

People connect to your most ordinary traits, blended up into a unique combination that is perfectly imperfect, distinctly you. Special accomplishments go out the window. Your pride and joy, may that be your job or stellar grades, are not what people love about you.

We get hooked on the ordinary. The thing that people will miss most about you when you're gone, is actually just your own peculiar, unique combination of quirks that probably aren't that quirky after all.

I take solace in the fact that none of us are really that special. Schafler even tells us to embrace it, in ourselves and in others. Real connection is born from an array of little things put together like a puzzle. Because, she reminds us, the best parts of life are hidden in plain sight. We just need to open up our eyes, and our hearts.

The crow's feet surrounding your eyes. The way you color-code your calendar. That peculiar method you have of loading dishes in to the dishwasher. How your right eye twitches when you get nervous. Your shitty handwriting. Those weird freckles on your cheeks. Now THAT is therapist-worthy, overly normal, aggressively ordinary love.

SECTION 3

'WE MET ON TINDER'

———

TALES OF TINDER DATES PAST

When I first got a Tinder, I put a cute blurb in my biography about how I loved poetry, being outside, and the taste of anything birthday cake-flavored. I was a Maryland local going to school in DC, interested in dining out, fine wines, and true companionship. It took dozens of matches and several messages from hookup-thirsty young men to change my biography to a Kanye West lyric and picture of me with a margarita in hand. It was then that I realized that this wasn't all that serious.

One-third of all new relationships begin online. How annoying that my parents always tell me to get off my phone...especially when I can name five couples off the top of my head who sprouted a relationship on an app like Tinder or Bumble.

When I first met Matt at Samovar tea house on Valencia Street in San Francisco, I was hesitant. Sure, he looked cute playing guitar in his profile picture, leading to an inevitable mutual "swipe right," but we had no mutual friends, and I was completely new to the city (and the Mission neighborhood we were meeting up in). So when I arrived five minutes early, I scrolled through my phone and secretly hoped he wouldn't show up.

Fast forward five minutes, and we're sipping iced chai tea on a bench. The tea house is much too quiet for my liking. I pray that the barista cannot hear our conversation, simply because it is dull and I realize quickly that Matt's saving grace must be his guitar playing. I don't know what else to say. I have no further questions, and I can tell that none of our interests line up. He isn't in school, he has no motivations, and his mother is paying his rent at his expensive high-rise while he seemingly goes on Tinder dates for a living. The date is quick and pain-less, with no physical interaction. I was pleasantly surprised. He just wanted to buy me tea and learn a bit about a girl who's new in town! No strings attached, right?

Wrong. He texted me a few nights later, asking me to come over in typical booty-call fashion. I ignore his message, block his number, and let a few of my friends know of the disaster date. We can laugh about it now; it's over. Bye bye, Matt.

"So, I'm guessing you guys just had different expectations, then. He wanted to hook up, you wanted to talk," one of my friends said. I was surprised. Why would he even ask me to go to the tea house, if he just wanted to reap the physical benefits? Sounds like a $4 rejection to me. Not to mention it was, like, 4pm. Not exactly booty-call time, if you ask me. I bet he didn't even play guitar.

Another instance of an online date gone awry is with Hunter, the sweet, southern boy from North Carolina who was studying in DC for a semester. We met on Tinder. I thought his main photo, which was a selfie with a goat with its tongue out, was funny. We exchanged numbers and texted frequently. He was easy enough to talk to, asking me how my night was (it was fine), what I was drinking (white wine), and whether I wanted to meet up later (to be determined, which would eventually turn into a yes). He had a sweet smile and nice blonde hair.

It was a rainy and cold February night. My friends and I had been having a girl's wine night, and he took a cab to the Georgetown campus. I showed him around, and he told me about his interest in politics and the government, which is what brought him to DC. Lessons learned from this date: try to deduce from an online profile whether someone voted for Donald Trump in the 2016 presidential election (spoiler: Hunter was eager to make America great again, or make Gianna uninterested again…whichever way you look at it), boys in fraternities need to mention their fraternity once every 15 minutes, and never trust a guy who owns goats. All important life lessons.

The internet is pivotal in the modern age of love. From dating applications, to Snapchat's ease of sharing photos, to even the coveted Facebook relationship status, online dating is slowly becoming the norm. Yes, in-person human connection will always remain desirable, but knowing that one in every three people we pass found their partner online shows the overwhelming power of this whole "Internet" thing.

But sometimes, in the midst of swiping on Tinder and meeting what could potentially be my next Matt or Hunter, I take a deep breath and remember that life is short. It will either work out, or be a great story to tell people. And usually, the stories involve free chai tea and a political debate on a Georgetown rooftop with a frat boy from North Carolina. And if that isn't love, what really is?!

NEIL AND MATT

"We met on Tinder, actually," Neil said, laughing. "It was even crazier when I met him in person at work later that week."

It was January 2016 and Georgetown Cupcake was doing its usual bustling sales. Lines out the door on 33rd street, call-in orders, and dozens of members of the confectionary cult visiting the bake shop each day. The manager, Neil, was only 20 years old at the time and was juggling his cupcake job with a full class schedule and an architecture internship. Love was the last thing on his mind.

"It all sort of happened so fast. I was doing my usual Tinder round, checking into the app and swiping on a few people. When Matt's face popped up, I think I literally gasped out loud."

Neil's coworker, Michelle, had been telling him about a cute new Georgetown Cupcake employee named Matt who was switching from the Bethesda to the Georgetown office. She was begging them to meet, and while they were set to meet organically later that week, the Tinder-sphere made it happen a bit sooner. Call it fate, if you will.

"I was stuffing my face with Thai food in our small back office. Like, mouth full of Pad Thai. It wasn't cute. I knew Matt was coming in, but not right at that moment. We had matched on Tinder at the beginning of that week, and we were both scheduled to work Saturday. I came into work and Michelle told me that Matt was working. I was really nervous."

For a relationship to work all you really need is two things:

chemistry and timing. But as the legend goes, and as Matt proved, timing's a bitch.

"I took my break around 3 right when he came in. There was a knock on the office door, and of course it was Matt. My mouth was so full of food, and he asked for quarters for the cash register, so I gave him some. I felt awkward not saying anything, since we knew of each other from Tinder and Michelle playing middleman, so I introduced myself then. Michelle was laughing her ass off because she knew what was going on. The next two hours, we were working and packing cupcakes right next to each other, but we didn't talk much because I was nervous. I was leaving at 4pm, so I came into the office and decided to write my number on a sticky note for another employee to give to him... and the rest is history, I guess."

Such a meetcute doesn't come without its trials and tribulations, though. Neil and Matt suffered the classic "commitment issues" that strike many twenty-somethings.

"We have been up and down for almost two years. There's really no other way to put it but 'it's been complicated.' At one point, there was a sense of false hope. I scared him with commitment at some points, and we'd break up. Or he'd surprise me, like his infamous cheese and wine spread on my birthday, and we'd get back together. He gave me a key to his apartment; I'd text him too often and he'd take it back. I always had a sense of what we could be. It became evident to him that I was more invested than he was, but then we would always end up back in the same cycle because he deep down had the same feelings but couldn't express them."

Neil's steadfast love and loyalty, coupled with Matt's personal life (he wasn't yet out to his parents and family), allowed for a roller coaster of a relationship. Sometimes, being honest about how you feel about someone can hurt you more than it can help you. Ignorance can be bliss. It's the fear of rejection, the fear of starting over.

"Now, he has finally started to realize that this is more than what he originally thought it was; this is love. We are now going stronger than ever."

ISABELLE AND CONOR

Swipe left, swipe right.

It's the familiar tale of millions of users of dating apps such as Tinder and Bumble. You download the app seeking a hookup, or perhaps even a boyfriend or girlfriend. Add some photos where you look particularly good. Include a short biography about yourself, maybe where you go to school and what you do for fun. Women will sometimes add an inspirational quote; men will usually add their height to dictate just how tall they really are. It seems to matter. You can add an anthem, that song on Spotify that really describes you. Maybe import your Instagram so they can see even more photos of you. Write a few more lines. Throw in some Facebook interests, likes, and groups you're in. Try to make it as comprehensively *you* as possible, set your age and distance preferences, and wait for the swipes to roll in. Pray for some matches. Repeat.

Dating apps have taken the millennial love scene by storm. One in three relationships begin online, many of which bred from a simple swipe right, double tap, or direct message. If you like the way someone looks online, perhaps you could like the way they look in person. And some people join the apps hoping for something more, like companionship or relationship, not just a meager one-night stand with Chad from the college over whose anthem is "I Love Kanye" by Kanye West.

Conor and Isabelle met on Tinder in early 2017, and have been dating for five months. They started chatting casually on the app, but once they met in person, they felt an instant connection.

"When I'm around Isabelle, I feel comfort, a good kind of comfortable. I feel like I can be more vulnerable and don't have to put on as much of a facade as when we first met," says Conor.

"I definitely agree that our relationship has gotten more comfortable. At the beginning, it felt like we had to savor every little moment together. Now I feel like there is more of a balance between spending time together and being functional human beings," Isabelle notes. Times have changed since they first met on the app, and even since they met in person for the first time.

"Honestly, I like how decisive Conor is. I feel like because he is so decisive and honest, I'm never concerned about you saying or doing something to be nice and not because you mean it. This being said, you know how to be honest without being blunt or rude," Isabelle says.

Conor has nothing but nice things to say about Isabelle, too. "I just really love how good of a listener and responder Isabelle is. I can tell that she is listening and that she cares because her responses are always thoughtful and relevant. We never run out of things to talk about."

ZOE AND SCOTT

Sometimes all it takes is four months of effort.

That was the case for hopeless romantic Scott, who was being interviewed by Brandon Stanton of Humans of New York for a completely unrelated topic when he let slip the details of his thoughtful proposal plan for his beloved Zoe. He knew his proposal had to involve movies, because Zoe loves movies so much. Scott loves trains. Zoe's family owns a frame shop. All of these small details mattered.

Scott edited a vintage Italian black and white film for four months. He changed subtitles, added dialogue, and tweaked it to perfection to resemble him and Zoe's story. He rented out a 60-seat theater, invited Zoe's closest friends and family, and popped the question... not withholding a few nerves of course. Fin.

YOUR INSTAGRAM AESTHETIC

Have you ever done everything to impress someone, except for *be yourself?*

Clara Dollar, NYU student and *New York Times* Modern Love essay contest finalist, sure has. Her Instagram and Facebook presence is so carefully curated to be a perfectly quirky, just-ironic-enough version of Clara. All to get Joe's attention, of course.

It can be so easy to develop a caricature of ourselves online. A good app that filters photos, some clever copywriting on captions, and some ironic memes are just a few ingredients to the recipe that was Clara's brand. Joe pointed it out, too, noticing that her biting posts portrayed a version of her—internet Clara—that did not always follow suit with the real thing.

Oh, the crazy things we do for love. We will spend hours cultivating a brand, editing and writing and perfecting as if the Internet is our final exam, and the class is called "How to make people like the Internet version of myself." Shocking that some people had to fall in love the old-fashioned way: without Tinder, sans Facebook, and even lacking modern day texting. But hey, if our parents can do it, so can we.

Or we could all just pull a Clara.

SWIPE RIGHT

My friend's sister met her fiancé on Tinder, and their wedding is set for next year. She went shopping for a gorgeous wedding gown, planned festivities, sent out invitation, and even donned a celebratory cake with "Glad we swiped right" written in icing. It's safe to say she is proud of her digital romance; others cannot say the same.

Technology such as online dating and applications on our phones have not changed love. In fact, Helen Fisher reminds us in her TED Talk that love only has three ingredients: sex drive, feelings of intense romantic love, and feelings of deep cosmic attachment to a long-term partner. The presence of a dating app on your phone, or that Match.com profile you loyally update, does not change these three factors. Technology hasn't changed love, but it has changed the way we find it, cultivate it, and keep it.

The only real algorithm in this equation, Fisher notes, is the human brain. Sure, we can swipe any which direction, and tap the screen a bunch of times, but our brain is eliminating the bracket of potential mates—life's biggest prize—allowing us to be self-selecting and picky when it comes to love. Phones or not.

"There's no question that technology is changing the way we court: emailing, texting, emojis to express your emotions, sexting, 'liking' a photograph, selfies ... We're seeing new rules and taboos for how to court. But, you know—is this actually dramatically changing love? What about the late 1940s, when the automobile became very popular and we suddenly had rolling bedrooms?" she tells the audience. Think of what used to make you popular: maybe a good job, the best house in the best neighborhood, a cool Ford car straight off the assembly line. No one was worried about perfecting their online presence. No one batted an eye at someone they might not be interested in, but with Tinder, it's just so *easy*.

More than 50% of Americans have had a one-night stand

in their lifetime, a statistic that multiplies in the millennial generation. Call it reckless, but the ease with which you can find a sexual partner means it isn't a long game. You aren't gambling with the future, this is just for fun.

Fisher sees changes in marriage patterns, too. "Today's singles want to know every single thing about a partner before they wed. You learn a lot between the sheets, not only about how somebody makes love, but whether they're kind, whether they can listen and at my age, whether they've got a sense of humor." So maybe those Tinder or Bumble hookups aren't a waste. People are now taking their time to love. There's no rush, and if sex is a part of the balanced equation, we've all become really good at math.

Maybe the other 50% should get on board.

ASHLEY AND ANDREW

"Yeah, we met on Tinder," Ashley laughs. She's proud of it, thrilled to have met a guy like Andrew who loves her so unconditionally. In her mind, why does it matter whether they met on an iPhone app? At 21 years old, there are only so many ways to meet people, especially on a hectic college campus. Andrew, 22, feels the same, and the couple has been going strong for almost two years.

"Andrew and I met on Tinder! I had just gotten out of a bad break up with my ex-boyfriend, and was pretty heartbroken, so my friends told me to get a Tinder to make me feel better. I could make myself feel better with countless matches from guys. I was really going through a wild period. Andrew had just gotten out a relationship, too. We both weren't looking for anything more than a casual hook-up, but one night I received a 'super-like' from him on Tinder and I swiped right. So romantic, right?" Ashley recalls, laughing. The ability to "super-like" someone on Tinder basically mean you swipe upwards—yes, there are more directions on the app than just left and right—and the other person gets notified that someone thinks you're not just cute, but SUPER cute.

"The following weekend we met up at a fraternity, one that wasn't his, and we just hung out with all of our friends together. That weekend we literally couldn't be separated and one of the nights we pulled an all-nighter, just talking about what we wanted to do in our lives, and we realized we had the same values and beliefs. That was a big moment for us. I took us on our first date to the dining commons, which was hosting a brunch for Valentine's Day, because we were still very casual. I didn't want to take him to a big fancy restaurant right away. Anyways, fast forward a month later and he told me that he loved me and, I kid you not, I said, 'No you don't!' Best story ever, right? I had just felt that it was too soon, and there was no way he could've loved me right away. Oh, was I wrong. We started dating on March 10th, 2016, so it's been almost two years. I think we'd both say it's been the best two years ever," Ashley continues.

Two years later, Ashley and Andrew both feel more mature, like they're ready to advance through life. With college coming to a close, the happy couple is anticipating a tumultuous period with job applications, graduate school essays, but still a lot of love for one another.

Ashley is ready for the changes, though, because she knows Andrew will be by her side the whole way, making her laugh each day. "As we have gotten to know each other more we laugh a lot more. We also have become increasingly supportive of each other as we get closer to the next stages in our lives and the dream of staying together after college is quickly becoming a reality as we plan for our life together. Through these last few months, Andrew and I have been able to mature together. We have become increasingly proud of each other's accomplishments whether it's from a small quiz to a job acceptance. We have also become very independent from one another, and have realized that we do not necessary have to physically be with each other, but we are just better and happier people when we are."

Andrew chimes in, saying that his "favorite thing about Ashley is… everything. That's an easy answer, and it feels like a cop-out, but I find it true. If I was forced to choose one thing however, it is how good of a friend she is. She's so selfless and kind it's crazy. She is also definitely crazy, and keeps me on my toes, but that's beside the point," he laughs. "Ashley is so easy to just hang out and relax with."

"I think my favorite thing about Andrew is his positivity and his dedication to reassure his love for me. Since the day I told him that I wanted to be a doctor, he has called me 'Doc Wong' and when I asked him why, he said it's for positive reassurance, because he knew I would be a doctor one day," Ashley smiles. "He is always such bright light in my day, and has restored the confidence in myself that I thought I lost. He is a breath of fresh air, and makes the harder days in life dealable. On top of that, he never asks for anything in return, so I know it is truly genuine, and I could not be luckier."

YOUNG AND IN LOVE

MY FIRST BOYFRIEND

My first boyfriend told me he loved me in the middle of an episode of *Family Guy*.

Sure, it wasn't the most romantic thing ever, but I was 16 years old and I was *pretty sure* this was love, and his Old Spice deodorant made my teenage hormones spark like a flame. When I went over to Ryan's, it was my young adult safe space. No adults yelled at us to change the channel. We would flinch every time we thought someone was walking down the stairs. We even had an entire couch to ourselves in a dark room. It was in this dark room that I learned what love is…or rather, what it isn't.

Being "in love" when you're 16 is a bit contradictory. You don't really know anything about life. You have no responsibilities. Your fights consist of getting mad when he likes another girl's Instagram picture, or when he gets assigned to sit next to another girl in class. Your biggest argument is when he gets a better grade than you on a biology test, even though last month you beat his SAT score by 200 points, and these things really matter because love isn't a competition, but if it were, you'd win. That's what being in love at 16 was like for me.

Ryan and I started dating when I was only 14. It was a quick "romance," sort of funny to talk about all these years later. It was freshman year of high school, and I'm pretty sure he held my hand on Halloween when we were hanging out with our friends and that's really all it took. A week later, he asked me to be his "girlfriend" outside of the art classroom in the hallway. He told me he "loved me" a year in. These terms are in quotations because looking back, we were both so young and uninformed. It almost doesn't feel right to classify it as love.

But then again, at what age can it really be classified? I know some couples in their thirties who have less maturity than Ryan and I had at 17. Sure, the scope of what you could possibly disagree on is much smaller when you're a teenage, without children, a mortgage, or student loans to pay off. But sometimes it's all about the mindset. Nothing is more fun than critiquing relationships of teenagers, wagging your finger and schmoozing about how they're just too young, too emotional, and have no experience with the the 'Real World.' But when you're in the moment and it's the middle of AP exam season in junior year of high school and your *totally cute* boyfriend texts you that he loves you and that your butt looks *totally sexy* in those Victoria's Secret PINK yoga pants and he wants to take you on a *totally fancy* date to Cici's Pizza that Friday, you can't really think of anything else.

It's been years since Ryan and I have been together, but I've yet to have something so serious. Perhaps it's because I can't bring myself to be fully committed to someone yet, or maybe it's just that I haven't found "the one" at a ripe age of 21. Why waste your time with someone who makes you anything less than ecstatic, excited, and elated at all times?

I love the quote "If the love doesn't feel like 90s R&B, I don't want it." If I had to write my own version, it would probably say something like, "If the love doesn't feel like getting asked to prom by your 16-year-old boyfriend with an $8 bouquet of flowers from Safeway, despite getting mad at him for ordering the wrong color tie at Men's Warehouse a week before the dance, but you get over it and go with him anyways just so you can make out in the back of his Subaru Outback on your way to post-prom at the bowling alley, I DON'T WANT IT!"

AUDREY AND JOHN

Long distance is never easy, but it sure can be worth it.

"John and I met in China the summer after my junior year of high school. We were both there on a study abroad trip, and we instantly connected. We dated for I think two weeks in China, but broke up when we flew back to the States because of long distance. I was SO sad," Audrey said.

Even though traveling across the globe brought Audrey and John together, it took nearly two and a half years for things to be brought up to speed. Even though Audrey didn't think much of their short fling and was ready to begin senior year, everything changed with one phone call.

"It was John, of course. Last year on Columbus Day he called me and said he was going to be in DC the next weekend on the way to visit a friend at James Madison University. He asked if he could crash on my floor... it seemed random, but it wasn't entirely out of the blue. We had kind of been Snapchatting, and I would send him several Snapchats that I would also send to other people. He thought they were just for him, though. He thought he was special, it was kind of cute."

The constant contact that phones bring to long distance relationships can be a blessing and a curse. Audrey and John began talking regularly through Snapchat, texts, and FaceTime calls after the visit.

"We just hit it off again instantly, resurfacing all of the feelings we had years ago. We got back together after that weekend, and have been together for a year now. In fact, after that Columbus Day weekend, he was going back to New York University so I instantly bought a bus ticket to go to New York. Our relationship, it's always been long distance. We've never been in the same place. John is studying abroad in Shanghai right now, so he's back in China and the time difference can be really tough. As a light at the end of the tunnel, though, John is attending NYU in DC this spring, so we'll finally be in the same city. Even if it's only for a semester, that's enough for me."

Staying connected amidst country lines, state boundaries, time zones, and poor WiFi connection can really put a relationship on trial. Audrey and John's college romance, albeit complicated, proves that technology can bridge distance, at least for the time being. Audrey notes that it can be quite tough having a relationship with a screen. It can facilitate happiness when you need it most, but also make you miss your significant other in lonelier times.

"Now John and I are both 19. Since we're long distance, our whole relationship depends on technology, so it can suck not being able to be there with him all the time but we use Facetime, Snap, etc. to stay in touch making sure that were still connected."

ALEXIS AND VIN

Blind dates.

Cringe-worthy? Yes. Sometimes awkward? Definitely. Successful? Occasionally.

Being set up by friends who think you two would be "just perfect" for each other has quite low returns. The forced situation, contrived conversation, and mutual friend in the middle of it all can be a distraction to finding someone truly compatible. However, for Alexis and Vin, their blind date lead to an instant connection.

"We both go to Syracuse University. I'm 20, he's 21. So basically, his fraternity and my sorority have a huge party each year that is a weekend-long thing, and at the time my two best friends were both dating boys in his fraternity. I was joking that I'd have no one to hang out with at the event, so my friend set me up with his "big." We got set up on a blind date for the date party and we had an instant connection. But it took Vin convincing as far as commitment. He is a year older, so we are on different pages and stages of life, but he had never had it in his mind to get a girlfriend. All of his friends are single, so he was so hesitant whether he wanted to commit. Eventually, it just became time, and we've been dating for 7 months," Alexis says.

Alexis and Vin's story is one with several complicated paths. Take the blind date aspect, coupled with the college Greek life system, and add in the complicated idea of commitment in a college relationship. Hookup culture, if you will: the ability to go home with someone, hook up, and continue seeing them physically without any further connection. It has been around forever, but the Internet makes it even easier to find someone. With so many potential matches available, especially in a social fraternity or sorority where mixers are commonplace, committing to just one person isn't always ideal. It can be less emotionally taxing to just keep things physical.

Like every relationship, they aren't perfect. They struggle with classic modern-day relationship issues, stemming from an overdrive of information. Constant updates on what they're doing, the ability to location track on apps like Snapchat, and succumbing to the ever-connected culture that we see today in 2017.

"A lot of our issues stem from modern day problems. Either one of us will do things on social media, or things he sees on social media, and I can see who he's talking to on social media. The hookup culture causes issues because a lot of our peers refuse to be in relationships. In a college environment, nobody feels the need to commit. I do trust him fully, but the way our culture is, you never know."

But with any couple, there are some loving, sentimental aspects you just can't get from a one-night stand.

"Vin is definitely the type of person who lives in the moment, which I don't do, so he helps me realize that it isn't always about the future, it's about the now. I can always be in the present moment when I'm with him."

KATIE AND CODY

"Her smile. Her laugh. Her personality. There are too many things I love about you. You already know that," Cody said.

"I love his sense of humor. And his farts…just kidding, don't write that! Also how he always takes care of me even though I am really emotional. And I love how he is so nice to everyone even complete strangers, and how much he loves his mom. It's really sweet," Katie sings.

Katie and Cody have been together for four months, but they have a complicated past of being on and off for two years. But even so, the simplest of events can tie together to create a love story unique and special. Across country lines, through college drama, and amidst a hot summer on the Eastern shore of Maryland, these two are *so* in love. And being in their young 20s, their love is one that not many come by in an entire lifetime.

"We met on the beach in the summer of 2014 through friends, because our mutual friends Maria and Jackson were trying to hang out. My friend Meredith was there too, and we met on the boardwalk at night by the Jolly Roger's amusement park." Katie recalls.

"One night, Cody and I were hanging out and had to drive me home. I tried to stay with my friends, but got in his black blazer instead. I loved that car. It was one of our first times alone together. We drove up Coastal Highway and it was kind of awkward at first. We talked about school. I remember Cody thought my school, University of Alabama, was really cool, and he asked me a lot about the football team. He had a girl-friend at the time, but they broke up. Besides, Cody says he liked me when he was dating her, and I liked him right away."

From then on, Katie and Cody were inseparable. They hung out a lot of the time. Katie mentions that she would make ridiculous excuses just to see him. One time, she said she needed matches to light a candle, because she just so happened to use all of hers. Cody came driving up in his black blazer, ready to buy Katie her special matches. They searched all up and down Coastal Highway.

"In reality I didn't need matches. I just wanted to see Cody," she giggles.

Another summer evening brought the couple to the Sea Shell Shop. Their dates consisted of driving around, enjoying the summer air and the salty beach. But August was approaching, when Katie would head back to school, and Cody decided it was over. However, even when it was "over," the pair still talked every day.

Fast forward to 2017, nearly three years after Katie and Cody's tumultuous beginnings, they returned to the Eastern shore for their respective summer jobs. Cody was a bartender, and Katie worked at a bagel place.

"I was so nervous to see him when I got back. Cody texted me our first night and asked to go pick up his prescription glasses. I figured it was similar to my 'matches' situation and that he didn't actually need glasses," Katie smiles. "We've been together ever since. He asked me to be his girlfriend at the stoplight off of Racetrack Road by Crabs 2 Go, on the way to Walmart. I'll never forget that."

Katie tells the story as if we all know exactly where Crabs 2 Go is located. Her smile is contagious. I can tell that they are truly happy.

"I mean, he was going to ask me to be his girlfriend at Outback Steakhouse the day before…but his two friends crashed our date! So Racetrack Road sounded perfect to me."

GALILEA AND MAX

Galilea and Max sit down to spill their love story, and Galilea can't even get through the first few minutes without getting teary-eyed.

"I didn't know a guy like him could even exist. He is such a good person for me. He is so strong emotionally and I think when God made him, He was thinking of me," she says, wiping her eyes. The couple, both ripe at 22, have only been together for six months, and they both think this is just the beginning.

"We met when I was interning in Dallas, Texas in the summer of 2017," Galilea says. "He was working there because he goes to Southern Methodist University. One of the guys I was interning with, there were two of us, was rooming for the summer with one of Max's really good friends. My intern, his friend, Max, and a few other friends decided to split a table at a club in downtown Dallas, so my co-intern invited me. I go out that night, and I'm meeting everyone and I see Max, and I remember my first thought was "Who is THAT?" He was turned the opposite direction, and he didn't look at me, then I figured "Oh well. Not meant to be."

"The night goes on, I was dancing… and not thinking about us talking at all. I was just trying to have a fun night and make some friends for the summer. Then, he comes up to me to introduce himself and starting chatting me up. Someone ran into him and he spilled his drink on me! He was like, 'oh my gosh, I'm so sorry, I'll make it up to you, I'll take your shirt to dry cleaning.' I told him that I had another way he could make it up to me: show me around the city of Dallas, because I didn't have that many friends there, just living there for the summer. So he gives me his phone to put his number in it. Then I decided to see if he was actually trying to get to know more or just looking for a girl for the night, and I asked 'What's my name?''. His eyes got so wide! He was completely not expecting me to ask that. He nervously stuttered that he was "*soooo* bad with names." He was lucky he was so cute.. and I ended up giving me my number. He texted me later that night with his name so I wouldn't forget it, and I replied that it was nice to meet him, and that he still owed me a Dallas outing."

"The next day he texted me and asked to get drinks, and I remember thinking it was so weird because Georgetown has no dating culture, but he was calling it a date. I wasn't used to this. We meet at a rooftop bar and it was super romantic. At first, I thought he was such a player and probably did this to every girl, but a few minutes into our date there was an instant connection. There were no awkward moments, and our conversation just went on and on so effortlessly. I just remember thinking, "I don't want the date to end." So I started to ask him to show me around random places just to have more of an excuse to spend more time with him. He showed me the SMU campus, where he lived, his pool. At the end of the night, he leans in for a kiss and I instantly started over-thinking it. *"He's so cute, it's only the first date! He's already kissing me! Too soon. But he's cute!! Ah What do I do?* While these thoughts raced through my head, he kissed me. I over-think and he acts on impulse... somehow that's the only way we could've worked that night. He walked me to my car and tried to kiss me goodnight again. I leaned in and just as we were about to kiss I pulled back and said, "Work for it." "Okay" he replied. And that's what he spent that summer doing.

"He asked me on another date, and it was a summer full of getting to know each other, crazy date nights, exploring the city of Dallas, and growing closer each day. Our love grew and we decided to take a chance on people that we thought were worth it. Now we're going out, and have been long distance for months. In fact, in the past three months, I've only seen Max for 11 days. We're both just waiting for the next time we get to see each other and hoping for the day we get to be together for good."

Sometimes, meeting that one special someone can explain the reasons why it didn't work out with anyone else.

"Guys that I used to be with, they checked all the boxes. They were funny, same religion, same political beliefs, had the same sense of humor that only I laughed at. It was a lot of little things adding up, especially with one guy in particular who I thought was "the one". But one thing stands out with Max, he chose me. He saw that I was worth it like no one else before him did. He makes me feel things that I didn't even think were possible. I think that life is meant to be shared with one person: your soulmate. Thanks to Max, I truly do believe this is what life is about. Now... is Max the one? I don't know. But that's what we're both taking a chance on figuring out."

ALVIN AND DANIELLE

Alvin and Danielle, 20 and 21, respectively, met in church, a place where less that 1% of millennial couples have met their significant others in 2017. Odds stacked against them, their sweet love story has kept them in a happy relationship for eight months.

"We met at church, it's a Christian non-denominational church here in DC. I go to Georgetown, and Danielle goes to George Washington down the street," Alvin says. "So it was my first time going to this church, because I had just left my old one. My friend that brought me realized once the service was starting, he remembered he had to go teach Sunday school, so he left me left me there with Danielle, who he brought with him. I had never met her before, but we instantly connected. Meeting in church, we already had so many of the same views and beliefs."

"We started talking after that, but we didn't really get together until after she came back from studying abroad. We had made that decision before she left in case anything unforeseen came up. We met as sophomores in 2015, and she went abroad junior year in the fall. We got together spring of junior year, so we knew each other for a while before making things official."

"Our relationship honestly hasn't changed that much. We still do a lot of the same stuff, we are into the same kind of movies, and we're into cooking. It makes it so easy. She's a great match for me."

If you ever met Alvin and Danielle, you would instantly warm. Two sweet dispositions. This is what the world is talking about when it says "good people." They may only be 22, but their love is mature and wise. There are no texting games, no liking someone else's pictures and getting mad. No petty arguments or immaturity; impressive for two college kids in their twenties.

When asked what Alvin likes most about his girlfriend, his face lights up. He smiles smugly: "I love that Danielle is just very kind-hearted. When my friends from Georgetown meet her, they all instantly love her. She's so kind. Even if she doesn't have to be."

RACHAEL AND DEVINNE

Less than 2% of marriages are between high school sweethearts. Those tender teenage years birth a lot of relationships, as well as complicated trials and tribulations from college applications, attending different schools, and making it work despite being young. Rachael and Devinne were always great friends in high school. Rachael was the captain of the field hockey team, and Devinne, two years younger, was a football star. They shared friend groups, talked often, and always had a sweet spot for one another.

"We met in high school. We were in the same basketball class and would flirt all the time. I don't think either of us knew it would turn into something so much more," Rachael says. Five years later, their high school romance stood the test of time, college, and long distance. They're still together, with Devinne studying at Salisbury University and Rachael a teacher in the same county in which the couple attended high school.

Being together for five years, especially when you started dating in your young teenage years, doesn't come without changes. People mature, grow, and realize their full potential. Goals and dreams come to light, and part of growing up is deciding whether those future plans involve the other person.

Rachael, however, says that not much has changed in their love. "I think our relationship has only gotten stronger overtime. We have been through everything together. We started dating in high school and now I'm out of college with a full-time job. It is crazy to think that he has been there by my side through all of these huge milestones. A majority of our relationship has been long distance and I think that has only made our love stronger. I cherish the time I get to spend with him so much."

Devinne sees some changes in the maturity level and conversations of their relationship. "We have gotten closer and opened up more about our families and our feelings on specific things. Overall, we have just become more comfortable around each other. We have started to love each other more for our flaws rather than our perfections," he says.

Rachael's smiling personality and ability to light up a room makes Devinne swoon every time. "My favorite thing about Rachael is her companionship," he says. "She is always there for me whether its school work, making me food, or doing my laundry. She has always been a great helping hand and she is always looking out for me. I love her so much and I am so grateful for her."

Regarding Devinne, however, Rachael can't pinpoint just one thing. "It's honestly so hard to pick one thing. I love absolutely everything about him and I couldn't imagine my life without him. If I had to pick a few things would be his sense of humor, athleticism, his drive and ambition, and how much he loves his family. He always knows how to pick me up when I am feeling down. Devinne works harder than anyone that I know. He never gives up on himself and that is something that I really admire about him. Seeing him interact with his family is something that always puts a smile on my face. His little siblings look up to him so much," she says.

"Honestly, I could go on forever about him. I just love him so much and can't wait to hopefully spend forever with him."

MICHAEL AND PAYTON

Michael and Payton, both 21, have been together for three years. They don't have an anniversary, but instead both say that "everyday is an anniversary. It's a lot more fun that way."

The love-struck couple met the very first week of school at Georgetown University, and has been smitten ever since. Their relationship is full of maturity, wise musings, and discoveries about love that even the most seasoned of couples have yet to discover.

"Payton and I met the first week of school at New Student Orientation," Michael smiles. "There are a lot of stigmas in college about not dating right away, because people say to play the field and that sort of thing. Movies say that a lot too...college is the perfect time to sleep around. We both were attracted to each other and had a good connection, but we held off on being officially dating for a while. It was push and pull; one of us wanted to be together while the other didn't, until April of freshman year. Our relationship is traditional and old fashioned, especially for our generation. College students are under the impression that there can always be something better. But with Payton, I know there is no one better for me."

Payton laughs while thinking about how she met Michael. She begins, "At the beginning of every school year, Georgetown has an event called Club Lau where the library turns into a club. As a precursor, Michael and I never officially met for some reason. There he was the first night of orientation at a rooftop party, in the same vicinity as me. I shook Michael's hand and I completely wrote him off. He was in a rainbow bucket hat, a tank top with a picture of either the Virgin Mary or Jesus, and the shirt said #wasted. He was in cargo khaki shorts, knee high socks, and some rainbow Vans. I didn't remember his name. Our orientation groups were always in passing, and one day he waved at me and my friend asked who I waved at, and I had no idea who it was. Then, a few days later he winked at me and my friend said that it was Michael. I'll never forget this, the moment I realized that this kid deserved another chance: one day I was walking to the gym, and despite not being in contact for a while, he said 'Hi Payton!' and I was so shocked that he *still* remembered my name, weeks later. That night I got drunk and danced with him a lot. I told him he had to take me out on a date, and he did."

Dating for three years comes with a fair amount of change, too. "Things have been more real and serious lately. We talk about next steps and moving in together, and we involve our families," Michael says.

Michael adds: "On a deeper note, if I wanted anyone to know anything about our relationship or any relationship in general, I'd say that they're so much more difficult than I think they should be. People have a picturesque image of little fights that you get over, but we've had deep differences. When my parents always said it was hard, I didn't know what they meant."

Payton adds, "The reason I could never be without Michael is that he makes me laugh harder than anyone. Every single day. I think that's so important. I think laughing is the core of happiness, and we should make every day a happy day, and Michael does that for me. He is also very sweet. He understands me on a level that other people don't. He can read me a book and knows what I will think or feel before I do it. Having someone who understands you in that way makes navigating challenges a lot easier."

You can probably find the couple nursing a pitcher of beer at Georgetown's favorite bar, the Tombs, on an average night.

But this time, Michael is a bit better dressed than a rainbow bucket hat and #wasted t-shirt.

PAIGE AND JONATHAN

Cell phones are used to keep in touch, call one another, and in general connect two people. Well, Jonathan and Paige were brought together by new phones, but they didn't meet on a dating app or through texting.

"We met in 2014 at the Verizon store. My family went to get new phones and Jonathan was the worker helping us out. Right away I thought he was attractive and really mature. He left his business card in the box that had my new phone and on the back he wrote his personal number. I texted him to say hi and thank you, and from there we texted on and off for about a year. We were both in relationships at the time, but eventually we both became single and then we started dating," Paige explains. She's 20, he's 23. They've been together for over two years now.

"We started out as friends, so our relationship changed a lot when we started to see each other romantically and then started dating. The biggest change I've noticed is how comfortable we are with each other and how our love has changed. At first our love was feeding off of us liking how each-other looked and our personalities. Now I love him for his morals, his work ethic, how protective he is, his intelligence, and so much more. The more we got to know about each other, the more we found more things to love and appreciate," Paige swoons.

There are so many things that Paige loves about Jonathan. He treats her well, is caring, and has her back always. They prove other young relationships wrong with their maturity and ability to move past any small arguments. Paige excitedly talks about Jonathan: "My favorite thing about Jonathan—this might sound weird—but is that he reminds me of my dad. My parents have been together for over 20 years and are still so in love. I always said I want someone who treats me like my dad treats my mom, and Jonathan treats me with the same love and respect. His humor resembles my dad too. Jonathan also makes sure I'm staying safe, doing well in school, and that I'm happy with where my future is going."

Jonathan feels the same about Paige, too. "I love the way you look at me in the mornings when we first wake up. I love the way you look at me when I surprise you. I love the way you touch the back of my neck and play with my hair when I drive. I love you because you're willing to risk everything for me. I love you because you're my world and without you I'd be lost and empty. I love you because you always take my breath away when we go on dates and when you dress up. I love you because you always blow me away with how nice and loving you are and how you accept everything about me"

SYDNEY AND MICHAEL

Sydney's infectious laugh booms across the room. She's always the center of any joke, the first to make you crack a smile. Or at least, her boyfriend Michael thinks so.

"I'm 21, Syd's 20, and we've been together for a little over a year. She makes me smile and laugh so much, I can't imagine anyone else could feel differently," Michael says.

The pair, another college couple who made their relationship work amidst the hookup culture present at their university, is the perfect mix of old school and modern love. What better place to create a spark than a cabin in the woods?

"We met because we were both set up with each other for an away weekend for Michael's fraternity. Away weekend is where a fraternity rents a bunch of houses somewhere, in this case it was in the Shenandoah Valley for the fall, and all of the guys bring a date. Mike didn't have anyone specific in mind so he asked a friend of mine in my sorority to set him up. It seems like a weird concept because I didn't know him at all, and we went away together for an entire weekend but despite that we had so much fun together," Sydney smiles. The couple's pure happiness and ability to have fun with each other is apparent the moment they walk into a room. Sydney's disposition, huge smile, and classic belly laugh make her a magnet to anyone who walks by. And Michael…his smile says it all.

Despite being in tough college classes, and balancing even tougher extracurricular activities that make it nearly impossible to see each other some weeks, one year in the couple is just as smiley as their first weekend together. "Honestly our relationship hasn't changed much. I think because we were set up for a weekend, we got pretty comfortable with each other pretty fast. I think over time our love has grown stronger for one another and we now know what truly makes each other tick, but I think that is common in any relationship. We just know each other so well and I can honestly say that I have never been so comfortable with someone before. We can truly be ourselves," Sydney notes, confidently. The ability to be truly yourself with a significant other is sought after by many, and only sometimes achieved.

They've kept the travel trend going, too. Sydney and Michael love to take a scenic drive to the shore, where they spend their days kayaking or making smiley faces out of bacon. They're playful, the classic kind of love you see at a college tailgate and wish you could teleport back to being 21 and carefree.

"My favorite thing about Michael is that it is so easy to laugh with him. I have so much fun with him and his smile is electric. There is never a dull moment with him so I rarely have any bad days or bad moods when I am with him. He is just such a positive and kind person that everyone genuinely loves being around him. His take on life is admirable and inspires me to have a similar attitude," Sydney says, blushing.

"My favorite thing about Sydney is that every time I look at her, there is a different reason to smile and I find a new reason to love her even more."

APARNA AND MATT

At the end of the day, humans are just biological creatures. Sometimes, biology is exactly what brings you together. This was the case for Aparna and Matt.

"I'm part of a professional biology fraternity, and Matt, who transferred to the University of Maryland in 2016, decided to rush the fraternity in spring of 2017. We clicked immediately, and when we realized we had feelings for each other, we started dating."

Even though their collegiate Greek life love seems cliché, they've had ups and downs that have forced their relationship—and themselves—to mature in record time.

"Despite only being together for less than a year so far, we have definitely become more serious. Matt has a heart condition, and after an infection last semester, he had to spend three weeks at Johns Hopkins to cure his sepsis. As we both come from public health/biology backgrounds, we knew how severe sepsis was. I almost lost him, only after a month of dating. We both sort of realized that life is short and unpredictable, so it's important to make the most of each day and remind people often how much you love them. That's definitely contributed to why we've become more serious. We're in this for the long run," Aparna says.

"My favorite thing about Matt is that he's one of the most selfless people I've ever met. He rarely thinks of himself despite everything he's gone through, and he always puts other people first. According to Matt, his favorite thing about me is that I get him out of his comfort zone. I push him to try new things and put himself out there. Without my support, he wouldn't be driven to be the best he can be."

"What we like about each other is how similar we are! I know 'opposites attract' but it's so refreshing to be with someone who's always on the same wavelength as you. We seem to know what's on each other's mind and that's a connection we cherish."

NICKLAS

Nicklas and I met on the street.

No, not in some sketchy back alley, or in the darkness of the night. We ran into each other—physically, he bumped my shoulder and I gave him a snarky glance—and he told me how beautiful my eyes were.

It was Fall 2016 in Copenhagen, Denmark. The air was still warm, so I was wearing a beige t-shirt and was just leaving class to hop on my bike. A native Dane, Nicklas was meandering around town with his Danish buddies. They slyly pretended not to understand English, asking me if I knew where the nearest bathroom was. I saw right through their charade and smiled. It took about five minutes of flirty banter until he asked for my number, and then another week for him to ask me on a date.

Nicklas had jagged teeth—the braces trend never took off in Scandinavia—and smelled vaguely of cigarettes and cheap cologne. Regardless, he slightly resembled Harry Styles, and had strikingly blue eyes. I was captivated by our meet-cute situation on a hard-to-pronounce street name in Denmark. The whole encounter sounded flighty and spontaneous; the moment I agreed to go on a date with him, I knew this would make a good story.

Our first date was actually quite adorable. He said he had asked his mom for advice on how to impress "an American woman," and since I was new to Denmark, he settled on a quaint picnic in a rural town outside of Copenhagen. Of course, this was not without me spending over an hour commuting to the strange area, phone battery running low and funds on my transportation card depleting. Not my smartest move, but love's all about the risk, right?

Once I arrived in Hellerup, he picked me up in a small Volkswagen car that belonged to his grandmother. He drove me to a park, constantly running red lights just as they turned yellow. "It was purple!" he would laugh as he sped up. I assumed it was the only other color he knew in English. I still found it charming.

We laid out a picnic blanket, and he started to remove strange Danish foods from his Supreme backpack. He was really into American clothing brands, American music, and I suppose, American girls. He made me pronounce each of the foods we ate before I got to try them. He laughed at my mispronunciation of complicated characters and "potato-in-mouth" mumblings of the language. He spread an interesting fish product on some bread, and I struggled to make my tongue take the shape of a native Danish speaker. He kissed me during a Calvin Harris song. It weirdly felt like we were in a club, but also in a rural park outside Copenhagen. The kiss tasted like white wine and the Marlboro he probably smoked right before picking me up.

When he dropped me back off at the train station so I could embark on my long commute home, he kissed me and promised to come into the city soon. Sure enough, he drove to Copenhagen the next day for a night out on the town. We drank and danced like typical teenagers. One of his wealthy friends bought a table at the club, follow suit by several large bottles of expensive vodka. He put his hand on the small of my back, whispering that I looked amazing, that he wanted to dance, and begging me to 'please never leave Copenhagen.' I laughed, kissed him lightly, and pretended like we were Europe's biggest 'it couple.' The Calvin Harris song really came to life once again. He told me I was the most beautiful girl he had ever seen; I laughed and agreed.

I'll never forget our semester-long romantic fling, and I doubly won't forget his broken language and the time he said "the date were great" or "it were a fun time." He was cute, sort of dumb...and did I mention that one time he asked me to do his English homework?

MODERN ROMANCE

COPENHAGEN CONNECTION

"This... thing between us? It needs to end."

This was the funniest breakup I've ever received. He was 6'9,
Danish, named Tobias. Loved to fix bikes in our Kollegium
(a Danish apartment). Ate weird fish sandwiches on rugbrod,
would bike home from the bar drunk, and never wanted to
hang out with my outside of the apartment. Made fun of our
American accents (annoying), our fucked up political system
(understood), and our obsession with red Solo cups and shitty
beer like Natural Light (agreed). He was my tall, handsome,
Danish prince... but the love was unrequited.

Meeting someone while studying abroad was both my biggest

wish and my biggest fear. Wish, because then I would have a cute love story, a reason to move to Europe, and of course, a boyfriend. It had been a while, people. But I feared it because of the long distance, the expensive flights, and the inevitable breakup. Luckily, Tobias made it easy on me with a blunt phrase in typical Danish fashion: he ended it, a few nights before I left Copenhagen for good.

While our "love story" isn't exactly that, we had a few moments that made my heart feel warm. One night, I hosted a Christmas party and he helped me clean the floor. When all the other guests left to go to a bar, we stayed in the common area of our Kollegium and talked all night. His English was perfect, but he dreamed in Danish, and he often forgot silly words like "pet." He watched us cry during the presidential election, all of us American students staying up late because of the time difference, slowly watching states turn red, one by one. He didn't really understand it, but he tried to be there for me nonetheless.

The goodbye was tough. We both knew we would never see each other again, and it didn't really bother us. We had our fair share of sleepovers, cozy *hyggelig* nights, and Danish homework help. Our relationship would never cross the Atlantic. Heck, it would probably never leave our Kollegium building. But with Tobias, it felt right at home. His blunt, calm demeanor meant that nothing was a big deal, and everything could be easily solved over a pale ale or a smooth bike ride. Couple this with an anxious American girl living in a foreign country for four months, and I was eager to get inside his brain.

Love doesn't always need to mean something. Sometimes, it's a fluke. Other times, it's just for fun.

In the beautiful city of Copenhagen where the blue water sparkles and the colorful houses of Nyhavn line the harbor in bright hues, Tobias really knew how to keep things black and white.

36 QUESTIONS

Have you ever played 20 Questions with a friend, or maybe a love interest? Well, in a *New York Times* study, apparently the latest game is 36 Questions. The prize? Falling in love.

Okay, let's break this down. Most people believe that love can't be manufactured. *The New York Times* Modern Love column published an article that referenced a study with 36 questions to ask someone. Look each other in the eyes, answer the questions honestly, and the two of you should fall in love. Easy. Well, Mandy Catron is the postcard example of the study's success, and she talks about how she is still happily dating experiment partner in her TED talk. The science behind the experiment proved successful, as people so often love to ask her.

However, falling in love is not the same as being in love. Mandy warns readers, loyal 36 Questions participants, and those eager for a quick fix to love: falling in love is the easy part.

Think about it. You could love, or at least been fundamentally interested in, a variety of people. Maybe that cute guy from work with the striking green eyes happens to have the same music taste as you. When the two of you get to talking and realize the plentiful commonalities, BOOM. Love commences.

Or perhaps that quiet girl in your class has the same fears as you. She hates being alone and is incredibly claustrophobic. Upon taking note of this tidbit of information, the two of you hit it off and enter a fruitful relationship. Love, manufactured.

But, as author Mandy will tell readers, falling in love is as simple as 36 questions. Staying in love, though, is where it gets tricky. There are the complications of the mundane: once you start living together, the spice of a relationship starts to dull. The two of you need to do dishes together. You have to do laundry and figure out how to pay the bills. Things are no longer all pretty sparkling eyes and a shared taste in Fall Out Boy.

"The study does work, though. The participants feel closer after doing it, and several subsequent studies have also used the fast friends protocol as a way to quickly create trust and intimacy between strangers," she notes. Trust and intimacy can quickly turn into love. Throw in some physical connection, some vulnerability, and you've got yourself some romance. It's a simple recipe, really.

After falling in love is when the conflict arises. You have to deal with your partner's insecurities and doubts. You have to decide who deserves your love. You have to be ready to commit and really work at it like an ongoing project, not just a quick fix or easy answer.

Besides, love isn't multiple choice.

MADDY AND RYAN

Maddy and Ryan like to have fun.

So much fun, in fact, that their year-long long distance relationship doesn't even feel like work. So much fun, that even when Maddy gets back from her job as a teacher for Teach for America, juggling crazy kids and lesson plans in rural North Carolina, the first thing she wants to do is FaceTime Ryan and tell him about her day. So much fun, that their relationship never feels like work.

Maddy is lighthearted and relaxed. She grew up in Wisconsin with three brothers, and embraces a chill lifestyle. She never gets jealous and enjoys Ryan's company.

Ryan is a mechanical engineer, currently getting a computer science degree. He likes to brainstorm new places for Maddy and him to live in two years when Maddy's teaching position ends. They've mentioned California, New York, or even abroad. When Maddy goes to law school, she will go wherever Ryan is. The opportunities are endless.

"Ryan and I met in high school, but he was 3 years older, so I only knew his name. We both played soccer, of course, and we met at the alumni game two years ago in 2016 for our high school. After the game everyone usually goes out to the bars, so that night while we were out we started talking. He was going to walk me home...but instead we went for a walk until 5 am just talking on a park bench, his arm around me, chatting. It was cute," Maddy smiled, recalling their story. You know what Einstein said about relativity...put your hand on a hot stove for a minute, and it seems like an hour. Sit with a pretty girl (or in this case, a hot soccer player) for an hour, and it seems like a minute.

"He drove me home and two days later I left to study abroad in Denmark. He promised to take me out to drinks when I got back. I thought about him a lot while studying abroad, but didn't let it take away from the adventures I was having. The hardest part is that he doesn't live near me. I came home from Denmark and a few days before New Years Eve he texted me asking to meet up," Maddy recalls. She graduated from college in December 2016, just after getting back from Denmark. Swearing off boys and getting ready to prepare for a full-time job and potentially law school; Maddy was crushing it. But love, of course, works in mysterious ways.

On New Year's Day in 2017, Maddy and Ryan reconnected. They got drinks and hung out for a few hours, hitting it off again instantly. They are currently in a long distance relationship and Maddy didn't see him for two more weeks until Ryan planned a weekend-long date in Chicago, where he lives, to meet. She stayed with three of his random friends and had a day full of fun: Ryan had planned an adventure to a rooftop bar to see the Chicago skyline, one of the best in the world. They did touristy things, hung out with his friends, and ate deep dish pizza.

"We had the best weekend ever. That's when we officially started dating. I knew right when I met him that he would be around for a while, and I guess I was right."

When you know, you know. That's what Maddy swears by, anyways. Not just any guy can make you break a boy-fast, or commit to long distance after a semester of European adventures.

"We met in the summer of 2016, and once I got home from Europe it was pretty quick. We would hang out and talk all the time. We were both nervous about the distance, especially

Ryan having to travel back and forth from Chicago. We did a lot together that spring of 2017, because I worked and had weekends off. We would go to Indianapolis for the Indy 500, we went to Chicago, we came home to Wisconsin, and he came to North Carolina where I was teaching in July and August. We would take turns, like I went home to Wisconsin for a week to see him. I went to his family's Thanksgiving this year. When I met his mom at Thanksgiving, she said that I'm a keeper. That made me happy. He went to my family wedding, he's going to come to my family's Christmas. We swap; it's fun."

And fun do they have. Ryan is a free spirit, fun-loving guy; he's the perfect match to Maddy's laid-back lifestyle. Taking notes from this couple, anyone can learn how to sit back and enjoy each others' company. For example, Ryan shotgunned a beer with Maddy's brothers at her cousin's wedding. Her family gave the stamp of approval; Maddy says they really like him. She says he was so quiet the first time they met him, but now they always ask when they will see him next. Maddy has three brothers with whom she's incredibly close, so impressing the family is no easy feat. Ryan, however, got the job done.

As for how the happy couple manages long distance, they've basically become pros.

"We FaceTime a couple times a week, especially on the weekends. We text a lot at night, he writes me letters," Maddy describes. "He's such a romantic. Too good to me, for sure. We talk on the phone before bed. It's nice because there's no pressure to talk every day. Nothing feels weird. It doesn't feel like we've been away. We haven't really been in the same place but we have no boundaries or awkwardness. We have a strong trust for each other. We don't have to talk everyday, but usually we *want* to."

"We have iPhones, so we have shared albums on Photo Stream. Three, to be exact. One album is strictly photos of us two, and there's one album just of weird photos he takes of me. When we FaceTime he takes funny, weird pictures of me and puts them in the album. Strange pictures are a fun way to stay connected and keep our relationship fun when we're miles apart. Even when we aren't talking, or I'm alone in my house in North Carolina, he still makes me laugh."

"I actually said 'I love you' first. We were on my couch in North Carolina, in September the first week that my school started classes. I had been thinking about it, and I knew he loved me, I could just tell. I knew it would take him a while to say it, so I decided to woman up. I told him, 'this is going to freak you out, okay... I love you.' and he said, oh yeah, of course I love you too. It was really normal, and I feel comfortable around most people, but particularly around him. My job is so stressful and I have anxiety surrounding it, so the other night I told him I wanted to call him before bed, and he called me instantly, knowing that something was up. He usually knows what I'm feeling or what I'm going to say even before I do," Maddy explains.

The key to their relationship? Having fun together all the time.

"Ryan is just so fun. He is goofy and lighthearted. He doesn't make things complicated, and he doesn't act like he knows everything. When it comes to life, we like to roll with it. We like to have fun and be goofy, and I never feel like he's judging me for being myself," Maddy smiles.

Sometimes the little things make the strongest impression. This is especially true for Maddy and Ryan, a couple with many quirks.

"I love when we take pictures because he is taller than me, but he still leans back in pictures to seem even taller. I don't think he knows I notice it, but I do. It's really cute," Maddy blushes. "I first knew I liked him because when he tells a story, he laughs first, which is annoying because he has a goofy laugh. In the beginning I would always ask what was so funny, what was he laughing at?! But eventually I got used to his goofy laugh and knew a story was coming. He just is so funny, even in intimate moments. He doesn't take anything too seriously and takes it all in stride. I am extremely different than anything he's ever experienced… meaning politically. I have a lot of passions, and even though he has his own thoughts, he likes when I get excited or passionate about things. I like when he gets awkward about PDA but does it anyway. He will weirdly put his arm around me, but then get used to it."

"Ryan and I can talk about serious things, like feelings, or about life, fears, and the future. He doesn't know everything he wants to do in life, and it makes me feel better because we are figuring it out together. We're young. It's fun," Maddy explains. She has a laundry list of things she loves about him. "He gets super lovey when he gets drunk. He loves to give me piggy back rides, and he ALWAYS drops me. One time at the Indy 500 he full on dropped me on my back and I couldn't breathe, I was laughing so hard. I was on the ground, shaking from laughing. Moments like those make me love him even more. Everyone was asking if I was okay, but I was totally fine. It was hilarious."

Maddy is Ryan's first girlfriend. He's 25, she's 22. Like many young men, he had a lack of interest in commitment at first. He didn't want to grow up, and usually just lives in the moment. Maddy says that growing up is scary to him. Getting a girlfriend and moving across the country is scary to him. But going through it together makes it all okay.

Maddy smiles, recalling their fast beginnings. "After studying abroad, I had a plan to not date until I was done with law school. After Teach for America and law school, maybe then I would consider it. I said no dating for 5 years. And then Ryan messed up the plan and we started dating when I got back."

Even the most well-thought plans can be changed for someone else. No to-do list, calendar, or itinerary needed.

MINIATURE LOVE STORIES

Brevity is key when it comes to love and how it's shared. Here are some of my favorite miniature love stories collected from family, friends, and even Twitter. Because sometimes, less is more.

> "Loved him. Nearly lost him. Rebuilt it again. Never stop finding the good."

> "An hour stretched to two, three, four, x—until none at all."

> "I gave her my heart, and she gave me a pen."

> "Thought it was love, it was, he loved himself more than I imagined."

> "I remember the first time he held my hand. I love it still."

"Love is not about finding the perfect person. It's about being the perfect person."

"She gives me presents with her presence alone."

"What use is money when you need someone to hold?"

"If he won't, someone else will."

A 24/7 SINGLES BAR IN YOUR POCKET

"Today, if you own a smartphone, you're carrying a 24-7 singles bar in your pocket. As of this writing, 38% of Americans who describe themselves as 'single and looking' have used an online-dating site. It's not just my generation—boomers are as likely as college kids to give online dating a whirl. Almost a quarter of online daters find a spouse or long-term partner that way," author Aziz Ansari writes.

Love is changing, and Aziz Ansari will be the first to warn you. While some know him as Dev in Master of None, others cite his work in *Modern Romance*, his first book about—you guessed it—the changing world of love and the digitization of romance. Basically, with access to hookups in your pocket, or a date a few taps away, younger generations are never satisfied.

After all, Ansari's parents had an arranged marriage, and have been happily together for 36 years. The old statutes we know and follow, rules by which we abide, and adages from our grandparents about love are outdated. We are growing older. This Internet thing is really catching on. And while everything else is changing and evolving and innovating, who's to say that love has to remain the same?

MARRY MY HUSBAND

If you love someone, let them go.

When popular children's author Amy Krouse Rosenthal was diagnosed with terminal ovarian cancer, countless dreams of hers flew out the window. Fellowships she wanted to apply for, new books she wanted to publish, even watching her children walk down the aisle... but most importantly, her relationship with her beloved husband, Jason.

Sprouting from a blind date in 1989, Amy was at first hesitant and had low expectations. But by the end of dinner, she knew she wanted to marry him. Thirty years, three children, and several books later, Amy Krouse Rosenthal's future came to a halting stop with a terrible prognosis. With only weeks left to live, Amy decided to use her platform and her penmanship to make a dating profile for her husband. After all, her love for him holds so deeply that she can't imagine him being alone.

He's average height, a sharp dresser, a wonderful husband and even better dad. An apt handyman, a talented cook, an alternative music connoisseur. Jason is a seasoned traveler, the type of man who showed up to Amy's first ultrasound with flowers. Handsome, compassionate, and artistic. She'll miss looking at that face of his.

The heart-wrenching tale, published in *New York Times'* Modern Love column, preceded Amy's death by just a few weeks. But her legacy lives on, as does that of her and Jason's love.

"My guess is you know enough about him now. So let's swipe right."

OLIVER AND NATALIE

Music festivals like Coachella and Lollapalooza are well-known for being a fashion show of grungy outfits, a wild place to experiment with drugs and alcohol, and a haven to express yourself in the music you love the most. Not many people would think about finding love in such a place, especially where drunk people roam about, crazy fans sit upon one another's shoulders, and screaming fans flock in mob-like crowds. Oliver and Natalie, though, met at the Moonrise music festival in 2015. They attended with mutual friends, thinking it was just another fun outing. They both would attend the festival every year, but never met one another beforehand. Now, they've been together for more than two years.

Oliver: Our relationship has changed by us being more open with each other and up front about issues, we have also improved our communication.

Natalie: Our relationship definitely used to be more physical and just using Snapchat to communicate to being more emotional and actually talking to communicate things. We used to just go out together because that's how our relationship started but now we do other activities that are more meaningful. In the last 2 years we both grew up and our relationship did too. It went from being easy and convenient to difficult and more complex.

Oliver: My favorite thing about Nat is that she loves me unconditionally and likes me for who I am.

Natalie: My favorite thing about Oliver is that he is always funny and makes me and other people laugh. We are definitely opposites and he brings the best out of me.

BENCHES

It's never too late to start over.

In a silhouette by the love-story fanatics at Humans of New York, two unnamed people on a bench recount their happenstance romantic journey. The man's wife passed away three years ago; the woman had been married for 30 years but got divorced. The commonalities between the two sprouted a perfectly imperfect budding romance, clad with baggage: her ex-husband would only sit and home and watch TV, while her new beau preferred travel, exploring the city, and visiting museums.

When asked what they two did together, what did he reply?

"Have sex. We're still young."

Hearing about love stories from an older perspective is both humbling and saddening. Sometimes, the relationship is simply outlasted by a number of years. It's gotten boring, or there's no spark, or two people have just become *done* with each other.

But then other instances, death is the culprit. When your husband of 40+ years dies, it's hard to even fathom moving on and finding someone new. However, if two strangers on a bench in Russia can do it, and have it be broadcast for the entire Internet to see, other couples who've withstood the test of time can give it a shot, too.

Perhaps there isn't just one person we are meant to be with, but a multitude. Not fate, but a second-coming form of love. When in doubt, give love another shot, because you never know just who you'll find.

CONCLUSION

———

"Maybe our girlfriends are our soulmates and guys are just people to have fun with," quotes everybody's favorite, *Sex and the City*. Would it be really annoying to end a book about love and relationships by preaching that soulmates don't exist? Well, let's see.

Novelist Marianne Kavanagh nicely sums up romantic destiny, or the potential lack thereof, in an article for the Telegraph: "Where did it come from, this idea that fate will guide us to the one person in the world who completes us and makes us whole? Maybe we don't like thinking that life is messily random. Or we need a romantic way of describing intense physical attraction. Or maybe it's just shorthand for the kind of overwhelming emotion we don't quite understand."

Kavanagh makes an interesting point. Perhaps life *is* messily random. If there's one takeaway from this book, it's that you never really know when you're going to meet that special someone. Michelle didn't know she would meet Marc during her France escapades. Neil doubted that swiping right on Tinder would give him the boyfriend of his dreams. Oh, and my parents? Well, they *definitely* didn't know they'd be visiting that same crab shack two weeks in a row.

Plato is often accredited with "discovering" soulmates. The Greek tale, as old as time, recalls that humans once had four arms and four legs, but were too powerful, so Zeus split each of us into two. We were supposed to spend the rest of our lives finding our other halves.

Some people call bullshit. I mean, *really* Plato? The population is exponentially growing, and if we weren't with one significant other, we would probably be with another. Even if someone *were* your soulmate, the odds of meeting him or her during your limited time on earth are miniscule. Despite how happy someone might make you, is there someone who can make you happier? In a world with over 7 billion people, the chances are high.

There are people who view relationships with rose-colored glasses (like me!), and those who point right to the statistical improbability of it all. In fact, it's proven that us rosy folks end up getting the short end of the relationship stick. "People who implicitly think of relationships as perfect unity between soulmates actually have worse relationships than people who implicitly think of relationships as a journey of growing and working things out," Kavanagh writes.

That being said, after perusing dozens of love stories, learning the three places to meet your partner, and rolling your eyes at the fact that one-third of relationships now begin online, I leave you with this: Don't make a person your soulmate, make *life* your soulmate. The people you meet along the way? They're just stepping stones on your journey, just bricks on the path. The odds you meet "the one" that Zeus and Plato and even my dad were talking about are slim to none.

But the probability that you are alive on this earth, during the lifetime when Tinder exists, in this universe, and even reading *this book* right now? Now THAT sounds like a match made in heaven.

So go for it. Embrace the messy randomness of it all. Fall in love.

ACKNOWLEDGMENTS

Thank you to everyone who has been a part of the *How We Met* journey. I have wanted to write a book ever since I filled composition notebooks with my elementary school thoughts at age seven. This dream would not have come true without the dedication of many close family members and friends.

While writing this book, I had the opportunity to interview dozens of lovely couples. Thank you to everyone who shared their incredible stories. Every interview was an absolute pleasure. Each serendipitous story and heartfelt Tinder match brought joy to my heart and sometimes – okay, most of the time – tears to my eyes. This book would not have been possible without your openness to share intimate details about your relationships. And to every boy who inspired a personal anecdote in this book, needless to say I couldn't have done this without you.

Thank you to my incredible friends and family. Mom and Dad, thank you for inspiring me with your love and commitment to one another. Laina and Maria, thank you for being the greatest sisters and cheerleaders. Johnny, thank you for being my comic relief. Catherine, thank you for your thoughtful feedback. Gina, Katie, Josh, and Natalia, thank you for reminding me that the truest of love is found in best friends.

Lastly, thank you to Eric Koester, Brian Bies, and the entire New Degree Press team. You've helped me turn my dream into a reality, one love story at a time.

APPENDIX

Abrams, Abigail. "Divorce Rate in U.S. Drops to Nearly 40-Year-Low." *Time*. Last modified December 5, 2016.

Amadeo, Kimberly. "Valentine's Day Celebrants Spending More in 2018." *The Balance*. Last modified February 12, 2018.

Ferdman, Roberto. "There are only three ways to meet anyone anymore." *The Washington Post*. Last modified March 8, 2016.

Kavanagh, Marianna. "Do soulmates really exist?" *Telegraph*. Last modified August 9, 2014.

Krouse Rosenthal, Amy. "You May Want to Marry My Husband." *The New York Times*. Last modified March 13, 2017.

Morris, Sophie. "Romance Inc.: Why the love industry flourishes." *Independent*. Last modified September 22, 2008.

Schafler, Katherine. "The Surprising Thing People Talk About Most in Therapy." *Thrive Global*. Last modified May 29, 2017.

Yu, Christine. "When to drop the L-bomb, according to science." *Headspace.* Last modified November 30, 2017.

Made in the USA
Middletown, DE
25 April 2018